THE DREAM OF PROSPERO

D. G. JAMES

THE DREAM OF PROSPERO

Tratto t'ho qui con ingegno e con arte;
lo tuo piacere omai prendi per duce:
fuor sei dell' erte vie, fuor sei dell' arte.

OXFORD

AT THE CLARENDON PRESS

1967

Oxford University Press, Ely House, London W. 1

GLASGOW NEW YORK TORONTO MELBOURNE WELLINGTON
CAPE TOWN SALISBURY IBADAN NAIROBI LUSAKA ADDIS ABABA
BOMBAY CALCUTTA MADRAS KARACHI LAHORE DACCA
KUALA LUMPUR HONG KONG TOKYO

PRINTED IN GREAT BRITAIN

FOREWORD

I WISH to express to the Provost and the Professorial Board of University College, London, the gratitude I feel to them for their invitation to me to occupy the Lord Northcliffe Lectureship in 1965. This book is an expanded version of the lectures I delivered in the College last year.

I had for some time hoped that I might find myself, in spite of my avocations of those years, agreeably compelled, or at least instigated, to complement what I said in lectures I had delivered in the University of Oxford in 1950, and which were published under the name of *The Dream of Learning*. These lectures were occupied chiefly with *Hamlet* and *King Lear* in relation to Francis Bacon's *Advancement of Learning*. Bacon's book was published in 1605; and in that year *King Lear* had its first performance: it was this fact which gave me my cue; and I tried to see Shakespeare and Francis Bacon in comparison with each other as prophets and makers of the modern world.

What I had long wished to do was to extend my reflections on Shakespeare's tragedies to Shakespeare's last plays, still having the comparison with Bacon in mind. The Provost's invitation gave me the opportunity I required; but it will be seen that I have in fact confined my reflections to Shakespeare's last play, *The Tempest*: I have not spoken of the last plays as a group. It appeared to me that my purpose would best be served by this concentration; and in any case *The Tempest* provided me

with far more than enough to talk about in the brief
compass of four lectures.

I have called these lectures *The Dream of Prospero*. What
I have had chiefly in mind in giving them this title will
become clear later; but I thought also that by giving
them this name I might help to emphasize their continuity
with the Oxford lectures of which I have spoken.
'A dream of learning' was how Bacon described poetry;
and here I speak of the dream of Prospero: Prospero who
was *par excellence* Shakespeare's man of learning, and who
was without a parallel in the liberal arts; and it is Prospero
who dominates and gives order to Shakespeare's last play.

It will be clear to the reader that I have not been able,
within the limits imposed on me by these lectures, to
provide here a detailed survey of the play, and of all the
problems it must present to the scholar and historian. My
chief concern has been to provide what I may call a live
reading of *The Tempest*, made in relationship to the great
tragedies. To do this, I have in my first lecture resumed,
with due variation, what I said in *The Dream of Learning*:
it was necessary for me to do this if the second *Dream* was
to have its own life apart from the first.

For the greater part, the book consists of the Northcliffe lectures as they were delivered; but lack of time
made it impossible for me to read all I had written; and
since coming to America, I have extended that part of
the lectures which concerned itself with the Plantation of
Virginia. The stimulus I have received at Yale, and the
resources of the great Libraries of Yale, along with visits
to the Carter Brown Library of Brown University,

Providence, and to the Folger Library at Washington, at all of which I have received the greatest kindness, stirred me to treat at greater length what I had written about the beginnings of North American history. Chapter IV of the book is now pretty fully occupied with this subject; and if only for this reason, and in this connexion, it is a pleasure to me to take this opportunity of thanking my colleagues in the Department of English at Yale, and the Master, Fellows, and students of Timothy Dwight College, for the inexhaustible kindness they showed me during my stay with them for the session 1965–6.

Further, I have special reasons for expressing gratitude to Mr. Thomas Randolph Adams, of the Carter Brown Library, Mr. Herman W. Liebert, of the Beinecke Library at Yale, Professor Maynard Mack, the Chairman of the Department of English, Professor Edmund S. Morgan of the Department of History, Mr. James M. Osborn, and Mr. Louis B. Wright of the Folger Library.

In writing about *The Tempest* it is impossible not to be in the debt of many Shakespearian scholars. But I mention here only two. First, I am greatly in the debt of Mr. Frank Kermode's New Arden edition of the play, whose text I have used. I have greatly profited both from its admirable introduction and from its commentary. My reading of the play differs from Mr. Kermode's; but my obligation to him is not the less on that account. Secondly, I wish to express a general debt to Mr. Wilson Knight. I well remember, in the mid-thirties, coming, by a happy accident, upon his *Myth and Miracle*, and the aid and stimulus I received from it; and it is a pleasure now, thirty years later, to acknowledge a deep debt to the great passion, individuality, and insight which he has brought to his reading of Shakespeare's works in general, and of the last plays in particular. I think it most likely that there is much in what follows with which Mr. Knight will not agree; but again, as with Mr. Kermode, my debt to him is none the less.

I wished also to say that I was fortunate in the publication, during the time in which I composed these lectures, of two books from which I have profited greatly. The first is *The Discarded Image* by C. S. Lewis, a great scholar and a generous friend, whose loss to us all is inestimable; the second is Miss Frances Yates's *Bruno and the Hermetic Tradition*, a work of profound learning which I have found invaluable. Then the publication, late in 1965, of Dr. S. G. Culliford's *William Strachey* was a most fortunate event for me.

Finally, I express my thanks to Miss Sheila M. Evans, of the University of Southampton for her typing of the greater part of this book; and I am now also hardly less in the debt of Mrs. Alice Whitham, of the Department of English at Yale, who has typed those parts of the book which I have added and amended during my time in New Haven.

The University of Southampton
July 1965

1553 Timothy Dwight College
Yale University
April 1966

CONTENTS

I. THE END OF TRAGEDY   1

II. THE STORM   27

III. THE MAGICIAN   45

IV. THE NEW WORLD   72

V. THE DREAM   124

VI. THE MYSTERY   154

I

THE END OF TRAGEDY

ECAUSE of the quality and scope of his genius, there can be, in the entire range of human thought and art, no topic of discourse more exacting or more important than Shakespeare's last play. This would have been true of Shakespeare's last play if it were the last in a series to which the accident of death had put an end; but it is true in the highest degree when it has the marks and manner of a fully deliberated final creation and of a farewell.

It is believed by some that *Henry VIII*, which was certainly written after *The Tempest*, must be said to be Shakespeare's last play. That Shakespeare had a hand in the writing of *Henry VIII* there can be no doubt. That he wrote all of it there can be much doubt; and I am one of those who cannot believe that he did. But if he did, it would still be true that *Henry VIII* illustrates Shakespeare's genius either not fully exerted or in decline. But this cannot be said of *The Tempest*: few will deny that *The Tempest* is one of the profoundest and most majestic of Shakespeare's creations; and that it shows every sign of being given by its creator, in its treatment of human life, a summary quality and an air of finality.

Of the marks in the play of this conclusiveness I shall

have more to say later. But of one of these marks I wished to say something without delay. This is, that it is difficult, in observing or reading *The Tempest*, not to receive the impression that Shakespeare comes much nearer in it than in any other of his plays, including the other 'last' plays, to speech or doctrine. I have said elsewhere, in speaking of the last plays as a group, that they seem weighted with doctrine which, however, has its existence only in the body of the plays. We may judge this to be in general true of *The Tempest*; we may indeed say that, in the end, it is a power of reservation and not of utterance which wins the day in *The Tempest* and which causes us to be teased by silence, or at least by obscurity, in place of being pacified by clear statement or formula. Still, I think it is true to say that there is, running through the play, a vein of allegory; and that in *The Tempest* more than in its immediate predecessors we see allegory and doctrine breaking through, or better, straining, the texture of the imagination's creation.

At the same time, it clearly will not do to speak of *The Tempest* as an allegorical work; allegory provides, or is intended to provide, through and through, from beginning to end, a system of explicit significances; and this state of affairs is hardly, in spite of what I have said, to be found in *The Tempest*. Indeed, I would venture to add to this that the literary historian needs to be on his guard, in his study of *The Tempest*, against seizing upon what appear to be allegorical elements in the play and yielding to them an undue weight and value. The deepest significances of all may well be felt or perceived by other than properly allegorical means, and in places in the play other than those in which allegorical meanings or significances appear to break out.

What I have here in mind will, I trust, become clearer as I go along in my discussion of *The Tempest*. But having said so much, I wish to add that I am not unaware of what Professor Edgar Wind said in one of the chapters of *Art and Anarchy*. He complained there that didactic art is now viewed as 'a kind of monster, a hybrid of intellect and imagination in which art is sacrificed to the interests of reason and reason betrayed by the use of art'; and he went on later to record with approval Baudelaire's remark that 'there is something good in Chenavard's assumption; it is the disdain of prattle, and the conviction that great painting rests on great ideas'.[1] I should be the very last to deny that there is a profound sense in which *The Tempest* 'rests on great ideas'; and all that I shall have to say later on will illustrate this. But I prefer to call attention to some words of Ruskin, which Professor Peter Alexander has recently quoted, in which Ruskin spoke of Turner's last works. 'There was in them', said Ruskin, 'the obscurity but the truth of prophecy; the instinctive but burning language which would impress less if it uttered more, which is indistinct only by its fullness.' I recall also Goethe's remark to Eckermann that 'if the imagination did not originate things that must ever be problems to the understanding, there would be but little for the imagination to do'.[2] It may seem odd to base

[1] Edgar Wind, *Art and Anarchy*, London, 1963, pp. 53–55.
[2] 20 June 1827.

the argument on the need to keep the imagination in full employment; but it is true enough that poetry is not science or philosophy, and that it cannot be resolved into either of them.

I turn now from *The Tempest*, and, for preface to what I have to say about it, to Shakespeare's tragedies. I take *The Tempest* as embodying Shakespeare's maturest vision; I take *Hamlet* and *King Lear* to stand, together and in their different and pre-eminent ways, for the tragic vision which immediately preceded the creation of the 'Romances'; and I turn at once to speak of *Hamlet*.

2

Hamlet, more than any other play, has kept its place and power in the theatre; in the theatre of Europe, it has a classic standing beyond all other dramatic compositions. None of Shakespeare's plays has been so often acted in Great Britain or in so many foreign countries; and of no play, by Shakespeare or by any other, can we say, having regard to Great Britain, the United States, France, and Germany, taken together, that it has rivalled *Hamlet* in the attention it has received from producers and critics; in all four countries it has attracted the greatest producers and the greatest actors.

Many qualities of the play contribute to making it pre-eminent in the theatre. Dr. Johnson said that 'if the dramas of Shakespeare were to be characterized, each by the particular excellence which distinguishes it from the rest, we must allow to the tragedy of *Hamlet* the praise of variety': variety and diversity of character, event, and feeling. It is certainly true that *Hamlet* has the excellence of variety. Still, this is an ancillary excellence only, and no doubt there are other ancillary excellences; but the 'particular' excellence of *Hamlet* is hardly here. I turn from Dr. Johnson to Goethe, writing not so long after Johnson's death, and look at some passages in *Wilhelm Meister* which sum up a discussion which has been going on between Wilhelm and Serlo. There had been talk about the novel and its differences from drama. (I quote from Carlyle's translation.)

In the novel [it had been said] it is chiefly *sentiments* and *events* that are exhibited; in the drama it is *characters* and *deeds*. The novel must go slowly forward; and the sentiments of the hero, by some means or another, must restrain the tendency of the whole to unfold itself and to conclude. The drama, on the other hand, must hasten, and the character of the hero must press forward to the end; it does not restrain but is restrained. The novel-hero must be suffering, or at least he must not in a high degree be active; in the dramatic one, we look for activity and deeds.

Now, if this is so, it is certain that, so far, *Hamlet* partakes of the essential quality of a novel, not of a play; and its hero is declared to be 'endowed more properly with sentiments than with a character; it is events alone that push him on; and accordingly the play has in some measure the expansion of a novel'.

But this is only a part, or a half, of the argument which seeks to set out the peculiar power of *Hamlet*. The argument further runs that in the novel some degree of scope may be allowed to Chance; but that it must always be led and guided by the sentiments of the personages; on the other hand, that Fate, which, by means of outward unconnected circumstances, carries forward men, without their own concurrence, to an unforeseen catastrophe, can have place only in the drama; that Chance may produce pathetic situations, but never tragic ones; Fate, on the other hand . . . is in the highest sense tragic. . . .

Now *Hamlet*, it is said, may have the character of a novel by exhibiting sentiments and events, not characters and deeds. Still, it is in the highest sense dramatic and tragic by the ordering given to its story by Fate. Goethe's view of *Hamlet*'s 'particular' quality is then that it unites the quality of a novel in showing sentiments and events, not characters and deeds, with the most distinctive mark of drama and tragedy, the control of its events by an inescapable Destiny. It is not dramatic: it fails to give us *characters* and *deeds*; it is in the highest sense dramatic: it is Fate that draws the plan, and it can admit only of a tragic ending.

What Dr. Johnson said of the play is true and important. But Goethe here calls attention to a diversification in it of which Dr. Johnson seems not to have been aware: it unites in the highest degree and with supreme success the characters of the novel and of the drama; and here, Goethe appears to suggest, is, in respect of the form of the play, its distinctive and unique quality. Whether in fact Goethe here rightly renders the essential qualities of the novel and the drama, I do not now stop to ask. To do so is not at all necessary for my purpose; and without doing so,

I can invoke the great authority of Goethe in what follows.

Hamlet, then, exhibits sentiments and events, not characters and deeds; *Hamlet* is precisely a study in thought and sensibility, not in action. Action is what is denied to the hero; and conscience (which we may properly take in the sense of reflection and anxious thought) makes cowards of us all:

> *And thus the native hue of resolution*
> *Is sicklied o'er with the pale cast of thought,*
> *And enterprises of great pitch and moment*
> *With this regard their currents turn awry*
> *And lose the name of action.*

The name of action is removed from the hero's powers; the 'pale cast of thought' is what holds our attention as it held Hamlet's; and this 'cast of thought' is both the source and the controlling power of the plot: it is what gives to the play the distinctive quality to which I have referred. We are to behold the action of thought and sentiment in arresting action; and the tragic, in this play, is seen as the arrest of action which the spectacle of life creates in its central character, and all the consequences of this arrest for himself and for others.

We may speak, if we will, of Hamlet's character; but in truth Hamlet is a hero without character. The drama, said Goethe, exhibits character and deeds; but these Hamlet does *not* exhibit. Hamlet does not carry out what are properly deeds, and what is properly character is everywhere to seek in him. It is the very idea of the play that this is so. Removed from willed, rational action, Hamlet is all the more on this account the play's lonely centre, fixed and determined outside the executive order of the world's goings-on. The play must advance and be brought to a conclusion satisfactory to the theatre; but it must not be Hamlet who advances it or brings it to a conclusion: others must do that. It is events alone that push him on. In all that he can be said to *do* in the play's action, he must be a creature of passionate reflection, impulse, and feeling only. The life of reason must not show itself in the behaviour of a pre-eminently intellectual hero. To have given him character would have been to thrust him into the world of will and decision; and this must not happen. He had formerly been the courtier, soldier, scholar, the rose and expectancy of the fair state; but the character required for these roles he had lost, and in regard to it was quite down.

Now it is this play, having this predominant feature, which far more than any other play, has held the stage of modern Europe, and which may be said to be, in a pre-eminent degree, the classic tragic creation of our modern centuries.

3

I pass now to speak of another and closely related feature of the play of *Hamlet*. I mean the deep and sustained identification of the spectator with Prince Hamlet throughout its action; and I do not doubt that this identity is cardinal to the play's nature and to its great success.

Such an identification of the spectator with Hamlet can occur only because Hamlet is himself, in the greatest practicable degree, a spectator of the events which make up the plot: he influences these events only by his inactivity, or by action which is either an evasion of decision (as in contriving the play to catch the King's conscience and in his 'madness') or the working-off merely of his exasperation (as in his treatment of his mother and Ophelia). He is withdrawn, as far as may be, from the play's action. He is carried along by a course of events he is helpless to control, or does not wish to control, or which he determines only by impulse, exasperation, or evasion.

It is with a hero having this character, or lack of character, that the spectator is able to identify himself. He does not identify himself in the same degree with Othello or Macbeth; he sees Othello and Macbeth as one in a group of characters, and in varying degrees he identifies himself with each member of the group. He plays here the chameleon poet; he 'rejoices', in a sense I do not now stop to define, in all the characters, good or bad, who play their roles in the making of the plot. But in observing *Hamlet*, the spectator, thus identified with Hamlet, is at a remove from all the other characters, and sees them not with his own, but with the eyes of Hamlet; and this distances them from him, as they are distanced from Hamlet

The distance of Hamlet from the other characters in the play is indeed a condition of the relationship of the spectator to Hamlet of which I have been speaking. Hamlet's mind is naturally speculative and imaginative: it is rare

and estranged; and his intellectual and emotional condition makes the other characters in the play appear
chiefly as they affect the glancing, unstable shifts of his
own mind. Even Horatio, to whom Hamlet comes near-
est, remains a curiously shadowy figure: he appears, does,
and says little enough; he is a foil, in his steadiness, to the
unresolved and unpredictable play of Hamlet's spirit. The
other characters occupy places in the action at far lower
levels than Hamlet; in their different ways they are baffled
and exhausted by him; he is whimsical and exasperating
and cruel by turns; nowhere is he intelligible to them.
Loneliness both drives him and is sought by him; it is
here the condition of the tragic, and the means of the
spectator's identification with him.

I have been speaking of the spectator's identification of
himself with Hamlet, and of the relation of Hamlet to the
plot and to the other characters, which makes this identification easy and natural. But our identification of ourselves with Hamlet is not only a formal requirement put
upon us by the play. There is another and more material
reason for it; and it is in this other and more material
reason that we must see, above all, the cause of the great
success and fame of the play. What animated Shakespeare's
imagination in his creation of Hamlet was the spectacle
of the human spirit, in the face of the world's evil,
arrested in nausea, and having no religious or other
belief: and of the spirit of denial which rejects the world,
and all its values, and its deep corruption. Shakespeare is
here exhibiting a condition, not an action; a revulsion,
not a character; and the play's end can only be death.

4

Of the means whereby Shakespeare made out of a state of inactivity a stage masterpiece, I do not now speak. But it is necessary that I speak of his creation of a man in Hamlet's miserable condition into being the first tragic hero of all time. The truth is that the traditional doctrine of a tragic flaw is not at all applicable to Hamlet. Othello, Macbeth, Lear, all have, if we wish to force ourselves into an Aristotelian jacket, a tragic flaw: they have a kind of greatness but also palpable weaknesses: they must suffer our moral judgement on them. But this is not true of Hamlet. His state of revulsion from life, and his failure therefore to order his life and practice in accordance with clear beliefs, do not occasion in us *judgement* on him. Instead, we pity him for a condition which is the human condition, a wretchedness in the face of the world's inexpressible evil and suffering and of our ignorance. This condition is one we share with him and which above all else identifies us with him. There is here no cause for the exercise of moral judgement; we are confronted only with a spiritual condition. Here is no play of greatness and heroism, of the bold, even if evil, act: only a despair which must express itself in indecision, in exasperation, in meanness, in cruelty, in self-pity; and Hamlet shows enough of all these. He cannot make up his mind about what he should do; if we at all realize his condition, we understand that he cannot; and he must work off his exasperation on his mother, on Laertes and Polonius, above all on Ophelia: it is inevitable that he should do so; and his self-pity and self-exculpation must operate to create the image of a sweet prince living in too harsh a world: how could he do otherwise, to give himself some remnant of comfort in the face of death and the great mystery of it which he has been at pains to expound to us?

We are not here in the world's morality and judgement; motives are everywhere to seek. We neither exonerate nor condemn despair; we can only observe its twists and turns, its savagery, its subtle self-deceptions. The characters with whom Shakespeare surrounds Hamlet are helpless to pluck out the heart of his mystery; they cannot begin to understand him. But *we* need find no mystery here, if we can at all look candidly at the human world and at ourselves. We may not understand Macbeth plunging into hideous crime, or Lear's vast stupidity; there is nothing that prevents our understanding Hamlet. The erection, in the nineteenth and twentieth centuries, of Hamlet's character and behaviour into an unresolved or at best half-solved mystery, throws a powerful light on the state of human self-knowledge in these centuries. Here is the ultimate human condition, and we, like Hamlet, can contrive no escape from it. Like him, we are most dreadfully attended; and like him might count ourselves kings of infinite space were it not that we had bad dreams.

Here then is the open secret of the power of Shakespeare's play over us, and what has made of it the stage's first masterpiece. Here the mirror is in all truth held up to human nature: not, indeed, primarily to good and evil characters and ideas; we *see* little enough of moral excellence and evil in *Hamlet*, if we compare it with *Macbeth*, *Othello*, *Lear*; what we see in *Hamlet* is the *reception* of evil by Hamlet's mind in its mingled torpor and feverishness. Because this is so, the play is abstract and metaphysical; it shows us less the human world than the human spirit under the impact of the human world, and all the mind's helplessness and ignorance under that impact.

5

I have been saying that Hamlet, unlike Macbeth, Coriolanus, Lear, causes in us a certain suspense of moral judgement. Hamlet does not act in ways we condemn: we only understand him and are disposed from the beginning to exculpate him. We see him, as he sees himself, as a victim of evil, and fully understand his question, To be or not to be? We become aware of the wretchedness of his half-being, and see him stumbling, in his despair, ignorance, and therefore irresolution, between life and death. We are well aware, as Newman said, that the spectacle of human life is indeed a vision which dizzies and appals, and that it inflicts upon the mind the sense of a profound mystery which is beyond human solution. Hamlet's distraught state, and then his failure, do not surprise us; we may not properly blame him, nor do we do so. We give him admiration and pity, and are carefully directed by Shakespeare to do so; and nowhere does he do what we condemn. The deaths of Laertes and Polonius come not upon him; nor, still more surprisingly, does the death of Ophelia.

But when this is said, we also see to what end and consequence Hamlet's condition, from which he is helpless to
rescue himself, brings him and others. Goethe said that
Hamlet concerns itself with sentiments and events, not
with characters and deeds; and this is true. But then, when
we raise our eyes from the completed course of the play's
action, we ask, Is the choice then between Hamlet and
Fortinbras? Or again, between suicide and the infliction
of misery? Or again, is *accidie*, or a mental prostration,
the end to which the reflective spirit must come? Or may
we say, in answer to Hamlet's famous question, that
Being is indeed attainable by the human spirit, that man
may come truly to be, that is, if not to be immutable and
eternal, at least, in accordance with Christian belief, to
become a partaker of God's immutability and eternity?
Is Being indeed an alternative to despair and death?

I do not consider that it is merely speculative to say
that Shakespeare's composition of *Hamlet* marked a
climacteric in his mind's knowledge of itself and in its
exploration of the world. The dramatist is a craftsman,
and his play must carry the stage. But he is not only this;
and Shakespeare could have composed *Hamlet* only
because Hamlet's question was his also, as it is, whether
we realize it or not, the question of each of us. But how,
or by whom, is it answerable? There is the divine answer
of faith; and there are the endlessly human and conflicting
answers of philosophy. But how is the secular dramatist
to find an answer provided to him neither by religion nor
philosophy, and which Hamlet (who had no religion, but,
as we may suppose, much philosophy) was helpless to

find? *Hamlet*, with its despair and defeat, was not to be Shakespeare's last play. It might have been. Despair might have been the end. But if the answer was perhaps 'to be' instead of 'not to be', it could only come, if it was to come at all, by Shakespeare's turning from the distraught mind of Hamlet to look again, by a great labour of perception, at the world which distracted it. This is what Shakespeare did; and the great tragedies followed. I turn now to *King Lear*.

6

I speak first of the overriding difference between the two plays of *Hamlet* and *King Lear*.

I remark first that the evil which provides a beginning to the play of *Hamlet* is yet an evil which was perpetrated before the action of the play begins. Besides, it was an evil act, secretly confessed in a distressful prayer, but unknown to, and unsuspected by, all others in the play, with the exception of Hamlet himself, and of Horatio, who must play no part in the play's public action. The King indeed declares his guilt, in prayer, late in Act III; and by this time there is a cumulative certitude in Hamlet's mind that the King is indeed guilty. But no one else knows or appears to suspect (in spite of abundant provocation) that this is so. Hamlet's certitude is a private thing, he is alone in his vision of his uncle's evil; and of this he does not possess *proof*. Therefore the play is given a subjective, half-delusional quality; and Hamlet's increasing conviction of his uncle's (and his mother's) guilt has something of the character of an obsession which must half-overthrow his mind. Because this is so, we are in *Hamlet* above all conscious of the play and quality of Hamlet's mind in his state of lonely oppression by an image of evil private to him. Besides, as I have said earlier, we *see* in the play little enough wickedness. It is not only that Claudius has committed his crime before the action of the play begins. Claudius, in the course of the play's action, and like Hamlet himself, holds off and delays; he is not quick to violence, shows forbearance, would shed his evil if he could, elicits pity; he too must be hard put to it before he takes arms against his troubles. All this was necessary for what Shakespeare wished to do: it was less evil than the thought, the realization of it, which he was here defining, the image of it in the soul, and the distraughtness it must bring with it. And, because it shows itself little enough in the play's action or in the behaviour of Claudius as we behold him, evil acquires in Hamlet's mind a huge, vague, metaphysical reality which dominates the play, extends far beyond Claudius and the Queen, and in the face and presence of which Hamlet appears small, helpless, and doomed. What obsesses Hamlet's mind is a power of evil which far exceeds the Claudius we see; it is anterior to the play's action, the hidden source of it, disclosed superabundantly to Hamlet, unguessed at by all others, but encompassing everybody and everything. It is this which fills the mind of Hamlet: a sense of a hideous, inescapable corruption of human existence, of which the world shows itself, as it always does, strangely unaware.

But if, in *Hamlet*, we *see* little enough evil, we see it in titanic proportions in *King Lear*. In *Hamlet* evil is above all an obsessive vision; in *Lear* it is a visible power which has everywhere the initiative and driving force of the play's action. In *Hamlet* we see a mind distraught by the realization of evil; in *Lear* we see the detailed action of evil wounding the mind. We are in *Hamlet* above all aware of the play of Hamlet's mind which must delay the plot's action; in *King Lear* we are chiefly aware of the play of evil itself hurrying the plot forward. In either case the issue must be disastrous; but in *Hamlet* disaster ensues upon a nausea of the mind and a failure of the will; in *King Lear* it ensues upon fierce, unquestioning action which Lear himself illustrates at the outset and instigates later in others. The one is a tragedy of the arrested mind; the other is a tragedy of uninhibited action.

I said that in *Hamlet* we see the human spirit stopped in dubiety, and then the failure of its will, before the awful spectacle of human life; but now, in *King Lear*, we turn to observe evil in action, from the mind sickened by the sight of evil to the spectacle which dizzies and appals it. I said too that, at the conclusion of *Hamlet*, there are questions to which Shakespeare provides no answers. We do not know, and cannot see, if there can be any resolution of Hamlet's condition, which is the human condition. But now that we are to behold evil, on a scale and having a fierceness unknown elsewhere in Shakespeare's writings, to what point will Shakespeare bring us? Will he now give us release from the prison of Hamlet's mind? Shakespeare's plays make up a single body of writing, and record in series the progress of his mind. They are 'comments', Keats said, upon the allegory of his life.

7

I remarked earlier, in speaking of *Hamlet*, that no good purpose is served by categorizing Hamlet as a tragic hero, having, in accordance with orthodox doctrine, his *hamartia*: Hamlet exhibits no *hamartia*, but a condition of the soul. Lear indeed initiates a tragic action by his pride and folly; he instigates evil in others; and this leads on to his own destruction. But if we look to the play of *King Lear* as a whole and to the story of Lear, we see Lear progressing from the darkness of the world's values into light. This is in accordance with no orthodox formula. Of Macbeth and Othello we may say that they are indeed men of natural nobility destroyed by evil in themselves and destroying others; they fit the pattern; the evil in them grows with the action and corrupts them and destroys them. But of Lear we must say that the evil in him gives way to innocence. To call him the play's 'tragic hero' obscures the play to us; we can only properly see him as delivered from the entire worldly values of his long, earlier life, and entering, before his death, upon a new existence. We must say of him that he manifests no process of moral corruption, but a transfiguration, through the dissolution of his 'madness', into a new life; and in this new life, blessing, forgiveness, and the deep mystery of things fill his mind.

But now, if we turn to compare him with Hamlet, we see that Hamlet's condition was one which, throughout his previous long, kingly life, Lear could not have known. But he came to it, or at least to a notable feature of it, in his madness; and in Lear's madness, we may say that Hamlet is re-born. Lear's 'Behold yond simpering dame . . . that minces virtue . . .' is Hamlet's 'You jig, you amble, and you lisp . . .'; it is the same nausea; and it reaches, in Hamlet and Lear, its extremity in its hatred of women. 'Give me an ounce of civet, good apothecary, to sweeten my imagination' is Lear's cry; it might have been Hamlet's. The sense of a total corruption of human nature came to fill Lear's mind as it had filled Hamlet's.

But now, in *King Lear*, this revulsion is seen as a feature of the development of Lear's mind. Hamlet, too, had suffered a sort of madness, a distraughtness of the mind to the point of its breakdown. He 'put on' an antic disposition; but it was not, we may believe, a fully deliberate putting on; it was a necessary, if intermittent, feature of his condition. Lear's 'madness' represented a still deeper injury of the mind; but it could not be, if only for the play's sake, what is properly an insanity; too much matter was mixed with its impertinency; and we never lose our sense of the true continuity, in spite of drastic changes, of the mind of Lear. Out of this condition Lear is recovered; and he is recovered in his beholdment of Cordelia. Women had been the chief object of the hatred of both Hamlet and Lear. Hamlet had driven Ophelia to madness and death. Lear rises from his grave to his vision of Cordelia in heaven. I said that Hamlet exhibits a state of the soul. Lear exhibits the states of the soul. Lear passes from the world, of which he had long enjoyed a full and passionate relish, to Hamlet's disgust for it and rejection of it. Then he is raised into a new life. Hamlet said he could be bounded in a nutshell, and count himself a king of infinite space, were it not that he had bad dreams. Prison became blessedness enough for Lear.

Hamlet, then, recurs in *King Lear*; he recurs more distressed, more mad; he also recovers; and in the world into which he is then born, we hear Cordelia say:

> *O look upon me, Sir,*
> *And hold your hand in benediction o'er me.*
> *No, Sir,* you *must not kneel.*

This is the world of which Chekhov said that it was one in which it would be strange not to forgive.

I said that Hamlet leaves us with questions to which no answers are to be found in the play of *Hamlet*; and I asked whether, in Shakespeare's exploration of the world in *King Lear*, these questions might find their answer. It might seem, from what I have said, that they do. But before affirming that this is so, it is necessary to turn to the plot of the play in which the progress of Lear's soul is set.

8

I have said that in *Hamlet* we *see* little enough evil. From the crime of Claudius all the action of *Hamlet* and the condition of Hamlet himself springs. But Shakespeare is at pains to delineate to us very clearly the state of mind of Claudius during the play's action. He does so in the half-soliloquy, half-prayer of Claudius in the third Act; and what we there see is one who would repent, pray, give up

his crown, his own ambition, and his power, but cannot:
a soul that struggles to be free, but is more engaged.
Claudius is in revulsion from his evil, but helpless to be
delivered from it; conscience makes a coward of him too.
We do not see this pitiable compunction of the wicked in
King Lear. Edmund, indeed, wounded to death, meant to
do some good; for the rest, evil in the play is sheer. Then,
over against Goneril, Regan, Edmund, and Cornwall, are
set figures of transcendent excellence and beauty, Cordelia and Edgar; and the play seems almost to acquire an
allegorical quality in its conflict of good with evil, each
pure, unmixed, defecated.

In this conflict Shakespeare nowhere mitigates the
suffering of the good, everywhere he exacerbates it. I leave
aside the main catastrophic events of the plot; and illustrate what I have said by speaking of Edgar and his father,
and of Kent and Lear. Edgar declines to disclose himself
to his blinded father where the plot provides no reason
why he should not do so, give Gloucester comfort and
succour, and save his life. But Shakespeare must make
Gloucester the inexpressibly pitiable figure we see on the
cliff-top, and subject Edgar to this misery. The natural
flow of Edgar's love for his father seems staunched to increase his own and his father's suffering; good itself thus
compels an increase of pain. Edgar later acknowledged
this for a fault in himself: he had denied to himself and his
father the joy they might have in each other except for
a last heartbroken, fleeting moment.

It is the same with Kent and Lear. Why did not Kent
disclose himself to Lear at the opening of the storm and

before Lear's madness set in? Again, the plot did not require that he should not; and again, Kent makes himself known to Lear only when Lear is too far gone in grief and desperation to take more than the barest note of him. In this way Shakespeare must isolate and deepen Lear's suffering, as he had Gloucester's. Shakespeare's mind is filled with a sense of the loneliness of suffering, and he must exhibit it to the extreme.

Then, towards the end of the play, Edmund is, at last, moved by his father's death to do good. But he knows that he has given orders to execute Lear and Cordelia instantly; it seems incredible that he should forget this; but he does so; and so, even more incredibly, does Albany. Here too, the natural action of good is forbidden. The tragic order of the world which Shakespeare here portrays must forbid it. In this order, virtue suffers merely, and suffers alone, and is helpless to arrest the power of evil.

When we come to the play's conclusion, we are provided with no tincture of comfort. It is true that the evil ones are destroyed, and that Kent and Edgar are not. But Shakespeare gives no sense of a continuing order, of a tragic episode which is concluded and done with, of an effected purgation. Albany declines the throne; it must fall, he says, to Kent and Edgar to rule the realm. But Kent has a journey to go; and the lines Edgar then speaks are filled with mourning. There is no word in them to rally our confidence and hope, such as were natural in other tragedies; and the lines are lame enough. We must 'speak what we feel, not what we ought to say', says

Edgar truly; and his last words look on to death, not life. 'All's cheerless, dark and deadly', says Kent; and so it is. In other tragedies the action is seen as occurring within the world's history; the action of *King Lear* has more the character of a metaphysical fable, exhibiting the human world in its fearful and disastrous totality.

9

I must now, in conclusion, relate what I have just been saying to what I said earlier about Lear himself. It is in the universe which I have just described that Lear comes out of the grave of his earlier world, and then of his madness, into his new life.

Now we are indeed accustomed to say that Lear is 'redeemed through suffering'. But to this, we are required to add that his 'redemption' only deepens the darkness of the world and sharpens its bitterness. The world is the more cheerless and deadly *because* Cordelia was what she was and *because* Lear became what he was at the end. It is idle to speak here of justice and mercy, or of an ultimate triumph of good. No such triumph is exhibited here.

It may be thought that a Christian strain appears to run in Shakespeare's mind in the fashioning of his plot, and in his delineation of Lear and Cordelia. He fashions his plot so as to show, as I have said, the extreme suffering and helplessness of love and its apparently hopeless defeat; Cordelia appears almost a heavenly figure of redemptive grace; blessing, forgiveness, and vision from another world come to occupy Lear's mind; and when Cordelia says

> *And wast thou fain, poor father,*
> *To hovel thee with swine and rogues forlorn*
> *In short and musty straw?*

Shakespeare seems here so to develop lines in the old play of *King Lear* as to invoke the thought of the Prodigal. Certainly, there is all this. But we certainly may not say on this account that it is a Christian play. Anyone not disposed to Christian belief can allow what I have just been saying: in candour he must do so; but he may still behold this strain of Christian perception occurring within a world exhibited by Shakespeare as irretrievably disastrous. There is indeed no demonstrable reading of the play, any more than there is of life itself. We may allow that it is possible that Shakespeare was indeed deeply committed to Christian faith, and that here, working within the limits imposed by the secular theatre, he was concerned to lead our minds to a sense of the Christian hope and trust. This may be so. But we must take the play as we find it; and we cannot properly say that it issues from, or manifests, or brings us to, a state of belief. We can at most say, with any confidence, that Christianity appears to move here in Shakespeare's mind as, in Keats's word, a 'speculation', a possibility, a hope even; but having said this, we must then go on to say that the play confronts us with unresolved mystery. We can also say, if we think of Cordelia, that she, and through her, Shakespeare, had come to a sense of life, and therefore of death, in which the soul makes no demand either of life or death. But there is no resolution here; there is only silence and darkness.

10

This, then, is the point to which we have come in Shakespeare's greatest tragic creation, which Shelley called 'the most perfect specimen of dramatic poetry existing in the world'. *Hamlet* may be said to be the classic tragic creation of our modern centuries, if we are to judge by the frequency of its performance. But Shakespeare advanced from *Hamlet* to *King Lear* to the final limits of tragic creation. Both plays have, more than any other play of Shakespeare, an ultimate, metaphysical quality, and a universal, symbolical power, exhibiting man in relation to his universe. I have tried to show in what sense *King Lear* may be said to represent an advance on *Hamlet* in its exploration of human nature and its world; I have also said that *King Lear* envisages spiritual achievement and conditions beyond the imagination of earlier plays; but I have also said that these achievements and conditions occur in a world exhibited as, so far as we are able to see, wholly disastrous. Dismay and despair can go no further than they do here. We cannot say therefore that *King Lear* answers the questions of *Hamlet*: instead, *King Lear*, in the form of its huge symbolism, remains itself a question to which no answer is provided.

Still, the last plays, and above all *The Tempest*, represent a new kind of dramatic creation; and I said of *The Tempest* at the outset of this lecture that in it Shakespeare appears to come near to speech and doctrine. *King Lear* is indeed a commentary upon *Hamlet*; it helps to explain it, and we are carried further. *The Tempest* is a commentary on *King Lear*. Of course, each play, as it came from Shakespeare's pen must stand alone, as an individual work of art; but it is impossible for us to conceive each as monadic. Each must take its place in the total exploration of man and his world by the writer of greatest genius in our modern world. I turn therefore now from *King Lear*, with all its storms, to *The Tempest*, in which Shakespeare's journey ended.

II

THE STORM

1

SHAKESPEARE called his last play *The Tempest*; and a tempest at sea opens it. The play was to end with a promise of calm seas and auspicious gales for a homeward voyage; but now, at the outset, we have storm and shipwreck. If we reflect on the themes traditionally ascribed to the play, reconciliation, redemption, forgiveness; on Caliban; on the marriage of Ferdinand and Miranda; on the journey home; we see that any one of a dozen titles might have served and been judged nearer to the play's progress. But it was the storm at the beginning, however quickly over and done with, which provided the title of Shakespeare's last play.[1]

2

The storm was a remarkable one. It needs little reflection to see that it was difficult for Shakespeare, if it was

[1] Shakespeare called the play *The Tempest* and not *The Storm*. I discern no deep significance in his choice of the word for his title; and there appears to have been little difference between the meanings of the two words. It is perhaps worth remarking that what we have in *King Lear* is, for much the greater part, called a 'storm'; but the word 'tempest' is used in *Lear* too (III. ii. 62; III. iv. 12 and 24). But in *The Tempest* the tempest itself is more frequently referred to as a storm than as a tempest.

easy for Prospero, to create and manage it. He must have thought of not staging the storm; it was bound to have difficulties for him and for any producer;[1] and he might have begun with Alonzo and Gonzalo and the rest already on the island and recounting their shipwreck. But Shakespeare wanted the storm and the shipwreck, we must suppose, for a physical presence and to fill the stage and our minds; in any case, Prospero himself had some recounting to do in the scene which must follow; and it would be too much if narration were employed in the first scene also. Shakespeare must have his storm, as, later, he must have deliverance from it. But the storm must not only cast the travellers ashore: it must be dramatic, serve economy, and aid the exposition of the situation we are to see treated in the body of the play. It must be of extreme violence in itself; it must also allow the Boatswain to be heard saying to Gonzalo: 'If you can command these elements to silence, and work the peace of the present, we will not hand a rope more.' This is not the language of men about to be shipwrecked. The ship is indeed soon to be wrecked; but we do not have continuously, throughout the scene, a sense of imminent disaster: if Shakespeare was to give us such a sense, he could not also have made

---

[1] I do not underrate the resources of the Jacobean theatre managers in producing shipboard scenes. Still, Gower, in the Prologue to Act III of *Pericles* says,

> *In your imagination hold*
> *This stage a ship, upon whose deck*
> *The sea-tost Pericles appears to speak.*

Besides, as Coleridge remarked of the storm in *The Tempest*, it gives 'the bustle of a tempest, from which the real horrors are abstracted'.

us see, as clearly as we do, the Boatswain, Gonzalo, Antonio, and Sebastian, nor made us learn that there are on board, beyond all price, a King and his Prince. Then, suddenly, the ship splits, and all is lost. It is here that the scene ends, with Gonzalo speaking of barren ground, long heath, brown furze, anything; we might think that all is not, perhaps, after all, lost. But Miranda confirms in the opening lines of the ensuing scene that the ship was dashed to pieces and swallowed by the sea.

But there is, later, another rendering of the shipwreck. Shakespeare could give this other rendering only after we have met Prospero, learnt of his magical powers, and of what he is about. Ariel had performed to point the tempest that Prospero bade him, and was now reporting to his master. He had boarded the ship, flamed amazement on it, in the waist, on the deck, in every cabin:

> *On the topmast*
> *The yards and boresprit, would I flame distinctly,*
> *Then meet and join. Jove's lightnings, the precursors*
> *O' th' dreadful thunder-claps, more momentary*
> *And sight-outrunning were not; the fire and cracks*
> *Of sulphurous roaring the most mighty Neptune*
> *Seem to besiege and make his bold waves tremble,*
> *Yea, his dread trident shake.*

In this terror, all felt a fever of the mad. The ship was afire; and all but the mariners leapt from it, Ferdinand first, crying, 'Hell is empty and all the devils are here.' The ship blazed; but it was not consumed, did not split, break to pieces, or sink. It was brought safely to harbour

and all its crew charmed to sleep. Those who had leapt
from the ship came safely to shore. Clearly, there were
two tempests.

Now of these two tempests, one is Miranda's (which
accords with what we have seen in the first scene), the
other Prospero's (which accords with what follows in the
rest of the play). We do not hear the full account of
Prospero's tempest until late in the second scene of the
first Act, where Ariel appears to tell his story. But at the
outset of this scene Miranda recounts to Prospero what
she believes she has seen. Prospero has yet indeed to hear
Ariel's report of the storm and the shipwreck; but he can
say, in reply to Miranda, that no harm has been done, that
what has been done has been in care of her and that there
was no soul—

> *No, not so much perdition as an hair*
> *Betid to any creature in the vessel*
> *Which thou heard'st cry, which thou saw'st sink.*

What Miranda believed she had seen was hallucination
only: the vessel she had seen sink was in fact safe in harbour. The natural storm and the magical, which Miranda
(and we in the first scene) thought we saw, and which
Prospero in fact contrived, were quite different affairs;
and it seems clear that this disparity, or contradiction,
was part of Shakespeare's intention in the play.

3

But I speak now of the opening of the play's second
scene which shows Prospero and Miranda talking.

Miranda's speech, with which the scene begins, is one of great beauty and inexhaustible interest. Its first lines are:

> *If by your Art, my dearest father, you have*
> *Put the wild waters in this roar, allay them.*

The rhythm of these two lines is one we have not encountered before in Shakespeare's writings: slow, entranced, sorrowful, strangely calm, as of a god observing, but hardly touched by, mortal pain.[1] Miranda had seen, or so she believed, the total loss of a brave ship and of its company, one of whom, at least, was noble; and she will recount in a moment the bitter distress she had felt in what she saw. But now, it is as if she were awakening from a dream, but calmly, and in the knowledge, or half-knowledge, that what she had beheld was her father's doing. The shipwreck she had seen had the quality of a vision or a dream which she might not break out from; and it is only now, when the loss of the vessel and its 'fraughting souls' is complete, that she pleads with her father to allay the storm. There had been, it seems, no question of her saving the ship by earlier appeal to her father. She only asks now, too late, that he allay the waters; she can only mourn what she had been powerless (as we must suppose)

---

[1] The lines as they appear in the Folio are

> *If by your Art (my dearest father) you have*
> *Put the wild waters in this Rore; alay them:*

where the brackets (with the words 'my dearest father' not easily spoken, or quickly) and with the semicolon after 'Rore' show clearly enough the speed at which the lines are to be taken. It is commonly agreed that the copy for the Folio *Tempest* was unusually good.

to influence her father to prevent. The calm of her opening lines comes from knowledge of suffering inevitable, irretrievable, finished.

Miranda's two opening lines may be said to have the rhythm of speech uttered between dreaming and waking. The 'dream' from which she had awakened had been a fearful one; but she does not at once go on to speak of it. She continues instead to speak of the still raging storm. Her opening lines, I have said, have no note of urgency or terror; nor have those which follow:

> The sky, it seems, would pour down stinking pitch,
> But that the sea, mounting to the welkin's cheek,
> Dashes the fire out.

It is only in the lines which now succeed that the rhythm of her speech begins to move fast and brokenly, as she speaks of her suffering in watching others suffer and perish:

> O, I have suffered
> With those that I saw suffer: a brave vessel
> (Who had, no doubt, some noble creature in her,)
> Dash'd all to pieces. O, the cry did knock
> Against my very heart: Poor souls, they perish'd:

Thus she re-creates the suffering she saw and felt; and then adds for commentary:

> Had I been any god of power, I would
> Have sunk the sea within the earth, or ere
> It should the good ship so have swallow'd, and
> The fraughting souls within her.

We observe that these concluding lines, after the tumult
of the lines immediately preceding, return to the meditative and composed rhythms of the earlier part of her
speech. We must not believe that, when she says that had
she been a god of power she would have saved the ship,
she speaks here in upbraiding of her father, who was
indeed a god of power, and who set the waters to bring
destruction and death. We cannot think that there is here
rebellion against her father; there is nothing here or elsewhere in the play to make us think so. But she knows that
Prospero *is* a god of power who might have sunk the sea
within the earth. She has indeed accepted his will; and
from this comes the composure of the beginning and the
end of her speech which encompass the suffering of the
lines between. But the 'amazement' she feels must be as
much on account of her father and his exercise of power
to bring destruction as on account of the perdition of the
ship and its fraughting souls. She is in the presence of love,
power, cruelty, suffering, and death which are all beyond
her understanding. 'No more amazement', says Prospero
in reply to her speech;

> *tell your piteous heart*
> *There's no harm done . . .*
> *I have done nothing but in care of thee.*

He loves her, has reared and taught her; she loves and
reveres him. But she comprehends neither him nor the
world he appears to command. He has destroyed the ship
and its company by his Art, and kept his child divided
between her anguish for suffering, her love and reverence

for him, and her incomprehension of his cruelty and
power. She is bemused and ignorant, lost in the face of
what she has seen and of her father. He has taught her
much, we are told; but what he is, and what she is, did
never meddle with her thoughts. Then suddenly, her
dream of human life, so limited and pure, is confronted
with shipwreck.

But in truth, the ship and its 'fraughting souls' had not
been lost. The direful spectacle of the wreck we see, in the
first scene, which Miranda saw, which other ships of the
fleet supposed they saw before sailing sadly home to
Naples, was an illusion merely. Or, so far as it had sub-
stance and truth, it must belong to a metaphysical order
not continuous with the succeeding action of the play.

4

The relation of the storm which opens the play and
which Miranda and we beheld, the human storm and
shipwreck, to Prospero's and Ariel's magical storm, is not
to be clearly discerned; there is strain and contradiction
here which Shakespeare was at no pains to resolve; and I
have just spoken of the storm and shipwreck of the first
scene and which Miranda beheld as belonging to a different order from that in which the rest of the play occurs.
But if we look now from time to place, we become aware
here too of a great vagueness. The stage directions, which
are unusually full and detailed in the text of *The Tempest*,
do not tell us where Prospero and Miranda stood to see
the storm and then to speak of it. The Folio text says

simply, before Miranda's opening speech in the second scene, *Enter Prospero and Miranda*. Modern editors have ordinarily envisaged them in this scene standing before Prospero's cave; and we may suppose that they have been standing there before their conversation begins. But it is not easy to see how, through the pitchy sky and the mounting sea, the shipwreck was visible to them, or, again where they could stand and speak in the still raging storm. Besides, we do not understand from the course of the scene that Prospero had seen the shipwreck. Miranda describes to Prospero what she had seen as to one who had not been with her as she watched. When Prospero speaks of the wreck, it is in reply to Miranda's account of it; and he says,

> *The direful spectacle of the wrack, which touch'd*
> *The very virtue of compassion in thee,*
> *I have with such provision in mine Art*
> *So safely ordered, that there is no soul—*
> *No, not so much perdition as an hair*
> *Betid to any creature in the vessel*
> *Which thou heard'st cry, which thou saw'st sink.*

For all that these lines say, what Miranda saw was an illusory shipwreck, as indeed it was; and when Prospero speaks later in the scene to Ariel, Ariel confirms to him that he had done all according to instructions given him by Prospero. Prospero's instructions certainly had not included the sinking of the ship and the loss of its company. It is therefore not surprising that the editors of the New (Cambridge) Shakespeare show Miranda, at first alone, before the cave, gazing out to sea; and Prospero then joining her, emerging from the cave. This will serve well enough, if we are willing to let Miranda, and then Miranda and Prospero, stand in the full force and road of the gale. Besides, we do not know when the storm ceases: we must suppose it does so when Prospero plucks off his magic garment, or when Ariel, singing, unheard by Prospero and Miranda, but heard by Ferdinand, 'allays its fury'. But we do not, and need not, when so much is visionary and ideal, worry our heads much about these things.

5

I said of Miranda that the shipwreck, somehow the work of her father, shattered her dream of human life. Her dream had been limited and pure; the ship she saw destroyed had, no doubt, some noble creature in her; and her vision of nobility, suffering, and death went closely along with her knowledge and love of her father. (Of Caliban nothing has yet been said.) It is as if suddenly she has come out of childhood and innocence; and now she is to hear her father speak, for the first time, of his and her history:

> *My daughter, who*
> *Art ignorant of what thou art; nought knowing*
> *Of whence I am, nor that I am more better*
> *Than Prospero, master of a full poor cell,*
> *And thy no greater father.*

More to know, said Miranda, had never meddled with her thoughts. This was at best only half true:

> *You have often*
> *Begun to tell me what I am, but stopp'd,*
> *And left me to a bootless inquisition,*
> *Concluding, 'Stay: not yet.'*

We may imagine that Prospero's broken beginnings of narration were his attempted replies to her unspoken wonder. But now she is to hear what she and her father are, and whence they came: and she must add to her new knowledge of the suffering of the noble a new knowledge of human evil.

Shakespeare exercises upon us, in the image we have of Miranda as she listens to Prospero's narration, his most consummate art. She does not look at Prospero, who doubts her attention. It is as if she has, again, fallen into a trance, and is moved out of herself by her new and fearful knowledge. Prospero puts off his robes, and says to her:

> *Wipe thou thine eyes; have comfort.*
> *The direful spectacle of the wrack, which touch'd*
> *The very virtue of compassion in thee,*
> *I have with such provision in mine Art*
> *So safely ordered, that there is no soul,*
> *No, not so much perdition as an hair,*
> *Betid to any creature in the vessel*
> *Which thou heard'st cry, which thou saw'st sink: sit down,*
> *For thou must now know farther.*

At a later stage, Prospero was to say to Ferdinand,

> *You do look, my son, in a mov'd sort,*
> *As if you were dismay'd: be cheerful, Sir.*

Here, too, is Prospero's serene reassurance of the young, and he gives it now to Miranda before he embarks on his story of evil. The direful spectacle of the wreck, which had moved the very virtue of compassion in Miranda, had been by him so ordered that not a hair of any head was lost. She was to hear now of another sea journey, which she herself had made to the island. But Prospero first evokes her remembrance of the time before, three years old, she came to his cell. *She* shall begin the narrative of what she is; let *her* remembrance begin the story. He will play the Socrates to his pupil.

> *Of any thing the image tell me, that*
> *Hath kept with thy remembrance.*

She replies,

> *'Tis far off,*
> *And rather like a dream than an assurance*
> *That my remembrance warrants. Had I not*
> *Four or five women once that tended me?*

We must imagine Prospero's barely supportable emotion when he hears this, and cries out:

> *Thou hadst, and more, Miranda.*

Then he goes on,

> *But how is it*
> *That this lives in thy mind? What seest thou* else
> *In the dark backward and abysm[1] of time?*

[1] The word was probably pronounced by Shakespeare as in modern French, *abîme*; it was indeed in the early seventeenth century pro-

I pause at this celebrated line. Keats underlined it in his copy of the Folio; he underlined also the line which comes later in this scene where Prospero speaks to Caliban

urchins
Shall, for that vast of night that they may work[1] . . .

Keats referred to both these lines in a letter; they haunted him, like the 'Hark, do you not hear the sea?' in *King Lear*. In the first, with which we are here concerned, we see the mind fetching out of its past some fragment of our infant dream—'of anything the image tell me'—stumbling in the vast darkness of what lies behind us, in the immeasurable depths which lie beneath us; a sense of the incalculable immensity out of which our lives appear and with which they are continuous, which we know, but cannot contain, within ourselves. (We think of the second of those last chapters of St. Augustine's *Confessions* which M. Gilson has called the *Paradiso* of the *Confessions*, and the words: 'Great is this force of memory . . . a large and boundless chamber. Who ever sounded the bottom thereof? Yet is this a power of mine, and belongs unto nature; nor do I myself comprehend all that I am.') Out of this vast darkness, Miranda brings the image of herself royally attended.

nounced to rhyme with time, but Shakespeare could hardly have intended that here. The word properly meant the 'great deep, the bottomless gulf, believed in the old cosmogony to lie beneath the earth' (*O.E.D.*); by the end of the fifteenth century it had come to be used to signify any deep or immeasurable space, chasm, or gulf.

[1] I keep the Folio reading, as Keats did.

> *Thou hadst, and more, Miranda. But how is it*
> *That* this *lives in thy mind? . . .*
> *If thou remembrest aught ere thou cam'st here,*
> *How thou cam'st here thou mayst.*

Prospero looks eagerly for some memory of the journey. But more, and of the journey, she remembers nothing. The break in her memory between Milan and the island was complete. Then the narrative begins.

Her father, twelve years earlier, Prospero said, was Duke of Milan. 'Sir, are not *you* my father? We must imagine Miranda turning in 'amazement' and fear to Prospero with her question. She had recalled four or five women that attended her; and some sense of her origin must earlier have moved in her mind. But now comes the thought that Prospero was not her father, and she an orphan. Then, quickly, comes the knowledge that Prospero, who ordered the sea and the winds, created terror and death, delivered souls unharmed out of shipwreck, was indeed her father, had been a King, and she his Princess. What dreadful calamity then had removed them from their royalty and brought them here? Her mind leaps to envisage evil to explain a king's fall from power.

> *What foul play had we, that we came from thence?*

This was her first strong envisagement of evil. But she recoils in rapt surmise to say, slowly,

> *Or blessed was't we did?*

Then Prospero's impassioned reply,

> *Both, both, my girl:*
> *By foul play, as thou say'st, were we heav'd thence,*
> *But blessedly holp[1] hither.*

Evil and blessing had gone together. Shakespeare will speak of blessedness: and elsewhere in the scene Prospero says that Providence Divine brought them ashore. But I add that a little later in the scene, Prospero says that 'Bountiful Fortune' has brought his enemies to the island's shores; and he goes on to speak of a most auspicious star whose light he now must court if his fortunes are not for ever then to droop. Elsewhere Ariel will refer to Fate, Destiny, and 'the powers'. Shakespeare will employ in these matters no fixed idiom.

Milan had been the first of the Signories of Northern Italy, and Prospero 'prime' amongst the dukes. Prospero makes clear that he had owed allegiance to no one: the Dukedom of Milan had been unbow'd to any dukedom or kingship, enjoyed absolute sovereignty. His brother, Antonio, next to Miranda, he had most loved of all the world. To him he had given the government of the state to which Prospero grew a stranger, 'transported and rapt in secret studies', the liberal Arts. Power corrupted Antonio.

> *I, thus neglecting worldly ends, all dedicated*
> *To closeness and the bettering of my mind*
> *With that, which, but by being so retir'd,*
> *O'er-priz'd all popular rate, in my false brother*
> *Awak'd an evil nature.*

[1] The past tense of 'help', used as a past participle.

Prospero's trust in him had had no limit; but it awakened in Antonio the love of power which Prospero had abjured. Antonio 'did believe he *was* the Duke', executed the 'outward face of royalty'; but then, to become, 'absolute Milan', to reach sovereignty, he gave up sovereignty and submitted himself, for sway, to the sway of Naples. This was the end to which his love of power had come: to yield up power, and *play* a duke merely. Dearly loved and trusted earlier, he is corrupted by power; he then gives it up, to retain its outward face. In the end he sought a shadow only: a shadow, he pursues shadows. Thus does Shakespeare render the story of power and its pursuit. Then, in order to give away his power, Antonio must remove 'absolute Milan'. To avoid (with, we must suppose, a dubious enough hope of success) the wrath of the people, who loved Prospero, he and his fellows put Prospero and Miranda out at sea, in a tempest. But the sea was merciful; and the winds,

> *whose pity sighing back again,*
> *Did us but loving wrong.*

Prospero had said that

> *i' th' dead of darkness*
> *The ministers for th' purpose hurried thence*
> *Me and thy crying self.*

But once embarked, he tells Miranda,

> *Thou didst smile*
> *Infused with a fortitude from Heaven . . .*
> *. . . which rais'd in me*

> *An undergoing stomach, to bear up*
> *Against what should ensue.*

Gonzalo strangely had been appointed master of the design; 'out of his charity' he provided rich garments, stuffs, and food; and 'of his gentleness' he chose and brought from Prospero's library books Prospero prized then, and prizes now, above his dukedom. Here to the island they had come, brought by 'Providence Divine', 'blessedly holp hither'. The story is over.

> *Now I arise;*
> *Sit still, and hear the last of our sea-sorrow.*
> *Here in this island we arriv'd; and here*
> *Have I, thy schoolmaster, made thee more profit*[1]
> *Than other princess can, that have more time*
> *For vainer hours, and tutors not so careful.*

This ends Prospero's narrative. But Miranda next asks,

> *I pray you, Sir,*
> *For still 'tis beating in my mind, your reason*
> *For raising this sea-storm?*

The tempest is still unexplained and a mystery to Miranda. Later Prospero was to seek to still his own beating mind. But now he will not answer, or only half answer, Miranda's great question.

---

[1] We may take 'profit' as a verb, 'to progress'; but also as a noun signifying 'profits of the mind', 'understanding'—greater than other princesses have ('can' = know, have skill in). I leave the Folio reading 'princess', a singular form of a noun ending in -s having a plural meaning.

> *Know thus far forth.*
> *By accident most strange, bountiful Fortune,*
> *Now my dear Lady, hath mine enemies*
> *Brought to this shore;*

and he speaks of an auspicious star whose influence may bring him to his zenith. Bountiful Fortune has brought his enemies to this shore. But this also she could not understand. She had seen, or so she had thought, the suffering and death by shipwreck of the noble; in fact, the ship, saved from destruction, had brought to the island, according to Prospero, only evil-doers. She had learnt, for the first time, the long story of human wickedness; she must now see, we are to suppose, its flesh and countenance; of any noble creature in the ship, a Gonzalo or a Ferdinand, Prospero had said nothing. But he had said that all was done only in care of her, his royal child. Here Shakespeare uses Prospero's art to give Miranda rest from her new and awful knowledge.

> *Here cease more questions,*
> *Thou art inclined to sleep; 'tis a good dulness,*
> *And give it way. I know thou canst not choose.*

But we are quickly to come to the play's ending—the present business which now's upon us. The long past will be resolved. But the play's action is not yet to be begun. There is more history to come first: we may meet the King's party only after the histories of Ariel and Caliban also have been told. But the histories of Ariel and Caliban are so much a part of the history of Prospero that I must speak first of him and of his magic.

III

THE MAGICIAN

I

BEHIND Prospero and his magic there lies a long, confused, and often tedious story of European thought and speculation. It is desirable, for a reading of *The Tempest*, to have some acquaintance with it; and I propose now to tell it, very briefly. Besides, there are in the play, lying behind and beneath the thought and speculation of civilization, deep primitive responses to human life and society, from which over the last three and a half centuries we have become increasingly removed, but which are still not beyond our imagination's reach; and of these also we must take account.

To do what I have in mind, I must begin with the philosopher Plotinus, who was born early in the third century A.D. I might have said that it is necessary to begin with Plato who had flourished seven centuries before Plotinus. But Plotinus and neo-Platonism must serve here for our beginning, and in any case, it is hardly possible to exaggerate their importance in the passage from the ancient to the Christian world. Before the first century A.D. was out, in the years when St. John's Gospel was probably being composed, there began a revival of Platonic thought which was to have immeasurable consequences for European civilization; it was this revival which led on to the work of Plotinus in the third century, and it was through the medium of the genius of Plotinus that the philosophy of Plato passed into the life and mind of St. Augustine.

There is a famous passage in the seventh book of *The Confessions* in which St. Augustine writes that he found in the writings of the Platonists the doctrine of the Divine Word, but not that the Word was made flesh and dwelt among us. No doubt Augustine needed to give a sharp twist to Plotinus's doctrine of the Divine Mind to see it as a prevision of the second person of the Christian Trinity. But my purpose now is to say that, like so much of Hellenistic thought in those times, the philosophy of Plotinus emphasized the religious and mystical elements in Plato's philosophy, and was always animated by an aspiration to divine knowledge and to a union through knowledge and love with the ultimate source of all being: it was a religion as well as a philosophy. Besides, it emphasized the theistical element in Plato's thought as well as the mystical; and the mind of antiquity may be said to come nearer to Christian theism in the writings of Plotinus than elsewhere.

But my purpose is less to observe the great debt of St. Augustine to Plotinus than to observe the deep difference between them. In the end, the important thing to say about St. Augustine is not that he was deeply in the debt of Plotinus; but that the appearance of Christian genius of the order which St. Augustine possessed was essential if neo-Platonism was to contribute to, in place of over-

whelming, Christian philosophy.[1] In the thought of
Plotinus we see, above all, a hierarchy of being ranging
upwards to the Divine Mind or Intellect which stands at
the upward limit of being; beyond it is the One to whom
being may not be ascribed nor quality attributed.
Throughout this hierarchy, emanations and influences,
fluxes and refluxes, sympathies and inter-animations, move
and work; there is a certain uninterruptedness from its
lowest stages up to its highest: it is an order not indeed
properly to be called pantheistic; but it is one which also
falls short of theism. The One of Plotinus is indeed holy
and alone and transcendent; but it is also beyond being
and personality, and therefore not to be identified with
the God of the Jews and the Christians. Thus, the One may
not be thought of as a creator, as the first chapter of
Genesis made St. Augustine think of a creator: the universe of neo-Platonism, said C. S. Lewis, speaking of
Macrobius,[2] merely 'seeps' into existence: 'where Christianity sees creation, neo-Platonism sees . . . a series of
declensions, diminutions, almost of inconstancies'. Again,
we may say that Plotinus, and in general neo-Platonism,
does not admit the category of the supernatural: the One
is beyond our thought, but not supernatural; and the
human soul does not appear in neo-Platonism, as it
certainly does in the writings of St. Augustine, as a
creature requiring a rebirth made possible only through

[1] See Etienne Gilson, *History of Christian Philosophy in the Middle
Ages*, London, 1955, p. 67, where he is comparing Victorinus with
Augustine.

[2] *The Discarded Image*, Cambridge, 1964, p. 67.

the action and initiative of its Divine Creator. These are some of the differences, which are greater and deeper than the similarities.

We have therefore a religious metaphysic in which the human soul is not to be seen, in Christian idiom, as 'natural' and able to be remade into something supernatural. Instead, it is a divine being capable of communion with the diviner forms of being; and because in this metaphysic the world of being is, with all its hierarchy and differences, of a piece, inhabited by a World-Soul which informs the universe in all its varieties of being, it lent itself too readily to theurgy, magic, and daemonology. The system of Plotinus was one of extraordinary elevation and purity. Plotinus did not indeed deny efficacy to theurgy and magic; the second and third centuries were too ridden by daemonic and occult belief for that to be possible; but he threw the weight of his noble influence against all practice which went along with these beliefs. The sympathies and correspondences which existed between the variety of many powers which went to make up the World-Soul allowed of such practices; but they did not belong to, nor were required by, the rational soul, which must seek its purity by prayer and contemplation.

But it was impossible that in those centuries this philosophical system, of great complexity and difficulty, and affirming no clear monotheism, should not, sooner or later, be turned into an alliance with magical and astrological practice; and we see this in the successors to Plotinus: Porphyry and Proclus. They indeed distinguished between theurgy and magic. Theurgy was magical practice turned to religious ends, using influences, oracle and daemon, and the occult powers of image and symbol, to the enhancement of the soul's purity and communion with diviner being; magic was the exercise of these procedures for profane and evil ends. There was to be a long history of this attempt to see and keep magical practice within the limits of the religious and contemplative life; and later on I shall speak a little of what was to happen when neo-Platonism came to life in Renaissance days. But already, in these early centuries, the Christian faith, from the mouth of St. Augustine, declared its abhorrence of theurgical as of magical practice. I need not here recount typical theurgical practices;[1] but it is clear that however much they might be related, and however sincerely related, to neo-Platonic religious belief, they represented an attempt to draw down and capture diviner powers, to put constraint upon the gods, and to exalt the human soul and its resources in ways intolerable to Christianity.

2

I have spoken of the hierarchy of being in the philosophy of Plotinus, ranging from the Divine Intellect standing immediately below the One, down through a universe which is informed everywhere, from the sidereal and planetary gods, through a daemonic order, to the human soul and to the merely material, by a World-Soul.

[1] The reader will find the last chapter of Professor E. R. Dodds's *The Greeks and the Irrational*, California, 1951, and an appendix in it on theurgy, greatly illuminating.

I refer now briefly to the place in this hierarchy, as it passed on through the Middle Ages into the Renaissance, of daemonic existences.

In the *Symposium* Socrates recounts what Diotima had told him of daemonic existence: the daemons—of whom Love is a great one—live somewhere between the divine and the mortal; and what Socrates says there, and what he goes on to say about the nature of daemons and of the men who can treat with daemons, was to have an immense and sinister influence in later centuries. God and man do not treat and converse; it is through the daemonical that God and man do so; and here, Plato declares, is the means and basis for soothsaying and goety. In neo-Platonist thought, daemons are located in the air, between earth and heaven. (Milton was to give them a place on the moon:

> *Those argent fields more likely habitants,*
> *Translated saints or middle spirits hold*
> *Betwixt the Angelical and Human Kinde.*)

They are embodied in matter of rare consistency, and are immortal, but not impassible, like the sidereal gods. But upon them fell, and if what Plato had said in the *Symposium* was true, was bound to fall, the bitter lash of St. Augustine. St. Augustine did not, indeed, deny the existence of daemons (or, as we may say in this context, of demons) nor of the power of magicians and theurgists to work marvels through their aid and agency; but he pronounced them all fallen angels and devils: he set over against them the holy angels who were the true instruments of God's Providence in the created universe, were the true 'daemons' and intermediaries between God and man, and who, in their celestial existence, were soon to be ordered by the pseudo-Dionysius into their historic hierarchy, from the seraphim down to the angels of human visitation.

As the Middle Ages went on, there were to be vaguely gathered into the daemonic family a great variety of spiritual beings, increasingly imagined as evil in their natures and influences, the stock in trade of magic and sorcery. Already in the fourth century Martianus Capella's *De Nuptiis Philologiae et Mercurii* gave account of beings between God and man, celestial, aerial, and terrestrial; they ranged from beings of the kind Plato had spoken of in the *Symposium* down to long-lived, though not immortal, dwellers on the earth: Pans, fauns, satyrs, nymphs; and we may add all the creatures of popular superstition in the Middle Ages and the Renaissance which Reginald Scot was to list in the *Discoverie of Witchcraft*, the urchins, incubi, witches, Robin Goodfellows, fire-drakes, puckles, fairies, and the rest. Besides, each element was to have its proper creatures of which Milton wrote in *Il Penseroso*:

> —*those* Daemons *that are found*
> *In fire, air, flood, or under ground,*
> *Whose power hath a true consent*
> *With Planet, or with Element.*

Everywhere, on the earth and up to the moon's orbit (and in some doctrines beyond it) there were daemonic and evil beings amongst which and under whose influence man lived his life. The terror of evil spirits did not begin with civilization, nor was it to end with the coming of it; and in the sixteenth and seventeenth centuries the human mind was scarcely less ridden by this terror than it had been in the centuries of the neo-Platonists.

3

In the celebrated revival of Platonism in Italy in the fifteenth century, the greatest figure was Marsilio Ficino, who was born near Florence in 1433. He worked under the patronage of Cosimo de' Medici to translate into Latin Plato and the neo-Platonist philosophers. But he did not begin with Plato. He deferred his translation of Plato in order to translate the *Corpus Hermeticum*, a body of writings, written by unknown Greeks in the second and third centuries A.D., of extraordinary elevation and nobility, typical of those centuries in emphasizing the mystical and theistical elements in Plato's thought, but notably influenced also by Jewish religion and thought[1] and illustrating thereby the advance of the European mind towards monotheism. Ficino translated these writings; he did not need to translate another and late Hermetic writing, the *Asclepius*, not included in the *Corpus*, which had been translated into Latin in an early century. The *Corpus Hermeticum* was singularly free of properly theurgical doctrine; the *Asclepius* was certainly not so, and

[1] C. H. Dodd, *The Bible and the Greeks*, London, 1954, pp. xiv–xv, and Part II *passim*.

suffered St. Augustine's impassioned condemnation in *The City of God*; but it was to have a profound influence on the neo-Platonism of the Renaissance. From translating the *Corpus Hermeticum* Ficino went on to translate Plato, some of the writings of Porphyry and Proclus, and then the writings of the pseudo-Dionysius and, after his famous meeting with Pico della Mirandola, of Plotinus. *He* was indeed to

> *out-watch the* Bear,
> *With thrice great* Hermes, *or unsphear*
> *The spirit of* Plato *to unfold*
> *What Worlds, or what vast Regions hold*
> *The immortal mind that hath forsook*
> *Her mansion in this fleshly nook.*

Ficino attempted to achieve a compromise between Christian beliefs, neo-Platonist philosophy, and Hermetic theurgical doctrines. This was a harder task than fell to Porphyry and Proclus in their labour to unite the philosophy of Plotinus with theurgy; Ficino had to deal with St. Thomas Aquinas as well as with St. Augustine. His purpose was to defend the forms of astrological magic, using talismanic signs and images, which aimed to draw down divine influence and power from the spheres and stars, and to avoid any charge of trafficking with daemons. But the result was confused and uncertain enough.[1] The result was still more confused in the writings of Pico della

[1] The reader will find Ficino's doctrines discussed in D. P. Walker, *Spiritual and Demonic Magic from Ficino to Campanella*, London, 1958, especially pp. 36–44. See also Lynn Thorndike's *History of Magic and Experimental Science*, Columbia, 1934, vol. iv, chapter LXIII.

Mirandola, who brought into the picture Cabalist magic, which might allow of commerce with the angels, to supplement Ficino's astrological magic. In his mind, as in Ficino's, there was an overriding sense of the difference between the magic that was evil and daemonic, and that which properly belonged to a Christian magus who might by charm and sign, music and incantation, draw down the influence of sphere and star for the divinization of the human soul. But his great *Oration on the Dignity of Man*, which exercised an incalculably great influence then and later, illustrated a philosophy, deeply in the debt of the *Asclepius*, which shows more clearly than any profession of magic by Ficino or Pico the spirit which underlay the impulse to magical practices and which must make all magic abhorrent to the Church. He began his *Oration* by quoting from the *Asclepius* the saying of Hermes Trismegistus that Man is a great miracle; and he then went on:

At last it seems to me I have come to understand why man is the most fortunate of creatures and consequently worthy of all admiration and what precisely is that rank which is his lot in the universal chain of Being—a rank to be envied not only by brutes but even by the stars and by minds beyond this world . . . (God) took man as a creature of indeterminate nature and, assigning him a place in the middle of the world, addressed him thus: 'Neither a fixed abode nor a form that is thine alone nor any function peculiar to thyself have we given thee, Adam, to the end that according to thy longing and according to thy judgement thou mayest have and possess what abode, what form, and what functions thou thyself shalt desire. The nature of all other beings is limited and constrained within the bounds of law prescribed by Us. Thou, constrained by no limits, in accordance with thine own free will, in whose hand We have placed thee, shalt ordain for thyself the limits of thy nature. . . . Thou shalt have the power, out of thy soul's judgement, to be reborn into the higher forms, which are divine.'[1]

So long as this spirit was abroad, it was not likely to continue to be constrained by any show of Christian belief. Cornelius Agrippa, who lectured and wrote in the early sixteenth century, was learned in the doctrines of Ficino; but his life and writings illustrate a return to Hermetic and medieval magic of a daemonic kind for which Ficino found no place; and his book, *De occulta philosophica*, was to be widely read in the sixteenth and seventeenth centuries. In particular, it was greatly to influence Giordano Bruno; and with Bruno we are in the England of Elizabeth, Raleigh, Marlowe, Sidney, John Dee, Shakespeare.

4

We see in the doctrines of Bruno the breakdown of the brittle alliance, in the writings of Ficino and Pico, of Hermetic and neo-Platonist teachings with Christianity. The religious Hermetism of the *Corpus Hermeticum* might be syncretized with Christianity, and there were Christian

[1] The translation of Miss E. L. Forbes in *The Renaissance Philosophy of Man*, edited by E. Cassirer and others, Chicago, 1948, p. 224. For a similar passage in the *Asclepius*, see Scott's *Hermetica*, Oxford, 1924, vol. i, pp. 293–5.

writers in the sixteenth century who sought to do so, like Ficino and Pico in the preceding century. But Bruno reverts to a neo-Platonism allied to theurgy, animated by the spirit of Pico's *Oration* in which man is created divine 'with the power, out of thy soul's judgement, to be reborn into the higher forms, which are divine'. The Faustian spirit in Bruno broke through any Catholic framework; he reaffirms the old doctrine of the World-Soul with its continuities and influences from the highest created gods down through daemon and element to the soul and the material; and magic becomes daemonic again, in a measure and in ways unallowed by Ficino and Pico. Bruno was no inaugurator of a new understanding of the universe; he goes back to the second and third century of the *Corpus Hermeticum* and the *Asclepius*. He was indeed modern in his vision of the abolition of the spheres and of an infinity of worlds; but this arose from no scientific understanding; it came out of the imperialism of human pride 'constrained by no limit'.[1] His imprisonment and death at the stake in 1600 was no consequence of his advocacy of the Copernican system (which he misunderstood); it came from his espousal of naturalistic doctrines and attitudes which the Church must find intolerable.

Bruno had been in England from 1583 to 1585, and had published in 1584 two of his most celebrated writings. *Dr.*

---

[1] Miss Frances Yates's book, *Giordano Bruno and the Hermetic Tradition*, London, 1964, provides an exhaustive and indispensable study of Bruno, and I am deeply indebted to it. See in particular chapters XIII and XIV.

Faustus was written at some time between 1587 and 1592. There is good reason to think that Raleigh and his School of Night provided a link between Bruno and Marlowe; and it is clear that Marlowe, who in his Cambridge years must have been acquainted with Italian neo-Platonist writings, suffered in the course of the eighties the impact of Bruno's passionate and peremptory genius. We do not indeed see in the author of *Dr. Faustus* a disciple of Bruno. Marlowe may have spoken in blasphemous ways which he shared with Bruno. But Bruno cannot be said to have been plainly irreligious, if he was certainly no Christian; and in Marlowe's play the spirit of Pico's *Oration* and of much of Bruno's writing is set in an unmistakably Christian universe.

Still, it is difficult not to believe that Bruno's 'heroic furies' did not help to inspire Marlowe to his. 'Behold now,[1] standing before you', Bruno wrote in his *Cena de le Ceneri*, published during his stay in England, 'the man who has pierced the air and penetrated the sky, wended his way amongst the stars and overpassed the margins of the world, who has broken down those imaginary divisions between spheres . . . which are described in the false mathematics of blind and popular philosophy'; and there is much more of this. But if Bruno's 'heroic' spirit aided Marlowe's 'heroic furies', Bruno is brought to earth in *Love's Labour's Lost*. We may certainly not identify Berowne with Bruno; but also, Berowne would certainly not have been possible without Bruno. Miss Yates, in her

[1] Quoted from Miss Yates's *Giordano Bruno and the Hermetic Tradition*, p. 237.

essay on *Love's Labour's Lost*, has called our attention to some lines addressed by Peele to the Earl of Northumberland, a conspicuous member of the School of Night, written about 1593, the year in which Shakespeare was writing *Love's Labour's Lost*. In Peele's lines Northumberland is

> *Familiar with the stars and zodiac,*
> *To whom the heaven lies open as her book;*
> *By whose directions undeceivable,*
> *Leaving our schoolmen's vulgar trodden paths,*
> *And following the ancient reverend steps*
> *Of Trismegistus and Pythagoras,*
> *Through uncouth ways and unaccessible,*
> *Dost pass into the spacious pleasant fields*
> *Of divine science and philosophy;*
> *From whence beholding the deformities*
> *Of common errors, and world's vanity,*
> *Dost here enjoy the sacred sweet content*
> *That baser souls, not knowing, not affect;*

and so the lines go on, deploring the time's lack of 'heroical spirits' and opposing wisdom and philosophy to the world's vulgar errors. Much of this comes from Bruno: 'thrice-great Hermes' is here, and Bruno's veneration for Pythagoras, the swollen pride of the mind, the contempt for the world's vanities, amongst which Bruno counted the love of women; and it is the spirit of Bruno as it animated the School of Night which Shakespeare treated in *Love's Labour's Lost*, and there gaily pricked its turgid nonsense.

5

We need not therefore be surprised to find it a far cry from *Dr. Faustus* to *The Tempest* and from the last frenzies of Faustus to Prospero's serene abjuration of magic and all its ways.

I shall later return briefly to Marlowe. I wish now, in the light of my disgression from *The Tempest*, to return to Prospero and his magic. I remark two things: first, that Shakespeare, in composing his last play, so grave and solemn in its purposes, was able to employ a magician for its central character to the enhancement of its gravity and solemnness; second, that, also, we behold in *The Tempest* the mind of Europe saying farewell to magic as a part of its imagination of the world. I shall speak in turn of these two parts of a complex and teasing situation in the history of Europe.

In presenting Prospero as a priestly, spiritual magician, Shakespeare was using a still living tradition. To speak for a moment of witchcraft, sorcery, and all forms of black magic, it is certain that it was now, when Shakespeare was writing, still a living part of men's imagination of the world. The power of witches and sorcerers to raise wind and tempest was everywhere allowed: one of Faustus's desires was to raise the wind or rend the clouds; and the storm which came down in 1590 on King James VI of Scotland and his Queen on their journey from Denmark was the doing of witches who were burnt alive, after confession under torture, in Edinburgh in 1591. There is no need for me to recite facts about the widespread and

horrible torture and execution of 'witches' in Elizabethan
and Jacobean England. Caliban's mother was a witch:

> *and one so strong*
> *That could control the moon, make flows and ebbs,*
> *And deal in her command, without her power.*

There was nothing unimaginable in this by Shakespeare's
audience; nor in Caliban's being a child begotten by the
devil himself upon a witch. If anything to do with
Sycorax taxed the credulity of Shakespeare's audience, it
was that in spite of mischiefs manifold and sorceries
terrible to enter human hearing, for one thing she did,
they did not take her life: they banished her only. She
would not, in Elizabethan or Jacobean England, have got
away with her life.

But if the sense of evil magic was still strong, so was
the sense of the use of magic for priestly and spiritual
purposes. The history of magic in European civilization
in its relation to the spiritual life in neo-Platonist times,
the revival of Hermetic and neo-Platonist thought in the
Renaissance, attempts in the sixteenth century to syn-
cretize these teachings with Christianity itself, provided to
Shakespeare the power to create as his central character
in his last play the priestly and spiritual magician dedicated to the bettering of his mind and seeking to order
events to the end of the purity of the soul. I said that the
De occulta philosophica of Cornelius Agrippa, published in
1553, was widely read and studied in the sixteenth and
seventeenth centuries. It was a confused syncretism of
magic, neo-Platonist philosophy, and Christianity: the

universe is composed of three worlds, the elemental, the celestial, and the intellectual; the influence of the Creator moves downwards through the angelic hierarchies in the intellectual world to the celestial world of star and planet and thence into the world of all of us; each world has its order of demons, from those inhabiting the intellectual world and having traffic only with the Creator, down to the daemons of fire, air, earth, and water; and the magus is he who seeks to ascend up through all three worlds to the Creator whose divine power he will secure. This syncretism was bound to be abhorrent to true religion; but it illustrates well enough the lively association which magic had with a form of religious aspiration in the sixteenth and seventeenth centuries; and it rendered possible the creation, in the early days of the seventeenth century, of a Prospero conceived as a holy and priestly magus,[1] whose mind was set upon divine things. James I's *Daemonologie*[2] (which refers to Cornelius Agrippa) distinguishes between magicians and witches; it condemns them both; but James seems to entertain towards magicians only a reluctant disapproval. They are at least inspired by a true curiosity, and are men of learning, and wish to come 'by not onlie knowing the course of things heavenlie, but likewise to clim to the knowledge of things to come thereby'. Certainly, the Devil leads them astray into 'unlawfull science'; but they appear in James's pages to represent in their intention a genuine labour after divine

---

[1] See Frances A. Yates, *Giordano Bruno and the Hermetic Tradition*, chapter VII, and D. P. Walker, *Spiritual and Demonic Magic*, pp. 90–96.

[2] Edinburgh, 1597.

things. No doubt, Shakespeare would keep King James in mind in his composition of *The Tempest* for a performance at Court in November; but he clearly did not think, and there is little or nothing in the *Daemonologie* to make us think, that Prospero would be offensive to the King.

6

But there is another side to all this, which I now briefly delineate. I remark first on the picture of himself in his days as Duke of Milan which Prospero draws in his opening narrative to Miranda. Milan, he said, had been the first of the Signories of Italy, Prospero prime among the dukes, and 'so reputed, in dignity'. Besides, he had been 'for the liberal Arts without a parallel'. Throughout the action of *The Tempest* Prospero speaks of 'my Art'; and by it he means magic; but looking back to himself as Duke of Milan his studies had been of the 'liberal Arts', amongst which magic was never accounted one. These were all his study, he says; he neglected worldly ends, was rapt in secret studies, and was all dedicated to closeness and the bettering of his mind; and it was his secret, close, spiritual life withdrawing him from affairs, which stirred evil in his loved brother. The Prospero Shakespeare here evokes for us, dearly loved by his people, is the recluse, the scholar, the saint; not the magician. The magician belongs to the island, not to Milan. Gonzalo out of his gentleness had provided for Prospero, on his dispatch into exile,

> *Rich garments, linens, stuffs and necessaries;*

there is no hint here of the magic robes or of the staff he is
to use in his exile. Books indeed Gonzalo provided:

> *Knowing I lov'd my books, he furnish'd me*
> *From mine own library with volumes that*
> *I prize above my dukedom.*

These were, we are given to think, the books of his
scholarly and spiritual pursuits. Later, on the island, we
hear indeed of his books in relation to his magical powers
but we do so from Caliban: Caliban sees Prospero's books
as the source of his power to compel spirits, and to seize
and destroy the books is the first requirement of the
conspiracy he leads. But Prospero, in renouncing his magic,
speaks of drowning his book. It was natural enough that
Caliban should see Prospero's books, embodying the
refinements of civilization, as the prime source of Prospero's power; but *we* are to think that the volumes from his
library which Prospero prized above his dukedom and
brought to the island were not textbooks of occult
practice; and if we do not know where his magic robe
and staff come from—and Shakespeare gives us no encouragement to think they come from Milan—we need
not worry either about the source of his book of incantations. It may or may not have been one of the books
Gonzalo gave him.

We are not then to think of Prospero coming to
Caliban's island accoutred cap-à-pie for magical plots and
practices. Besides, Prospero initiates no commerce with
spirits; he *finds* Ariel on the island, as he finds Caliban.
Releasing him from his torment, Prospero binds him to

years of servitude. That Ariel was on the island was an accident most strange, or a gift of bountiful Fortune, or of Providence: so it was that, years later, Prospero's enemies were brought to the vicinity of the island; and neither here nor at any point later in the play do we see Prospero engaged in magical ceremonies and incantations and calling up spirits to his service. The 'meaner fellows' whom Ariel employs in his tasks are at Ariel's command and not, at least directly, at Prospero's. It is true that Prospero says to Ferdinand, during the masque's performance, that it is being enacted by spirits which by his Art he has called from their confines; but the machinery of Prospero's magic is never made visible to us; and we see Ariel doing what he is commanded by Prospero to do, having, at his own control, the other and 'meaner' spirits, and free to exercise initiative in the detail of his tasks. Prospero's magical power is, of course, everywhere taken for granted: by us, by Ariel, by Caliban, and there is no gainsaying it; but we also nowhere *see* him as the magical 'operator'; he is kept clear of this indignity.

There was good reason why Shakespeare should proceed in these ways in presenting Prospero and his magic. It was relatively easy to show a practitioner in evil magic. Marlowe's Dr. Faustus rejects divine learning for what he calls the metaphysics of magicians; he goes into league with evil; he is shown practising his black Art; and at the end there will be the certain excitement of dispatching him to Hell. But the magic of Prospero is wholly good, and belongs to a learned, noble, and spiritual life. Shakespeare is careful therefore not to risk showing Prospero engaged in magical rite or in incantation. Besides, his magic belongs to the episode of his exile from Milan; it occurs between the committing and the righting of a bitter wrong, and in order to restore Prospero to his lawful throne and eminence; it belongs to the island, not to Milan; and the instrument of his justice, Ariel, Prospero finds there to his hand. Then, at the end, Prospero abjures his magic; it has served its purpose and may go; it is not necessary for the purpose he now seeks to fulfil, which is, as before, the bettering of his mind. Prospero is, we see, safeguarded by Shakespeare from all risk of the ambivalent associations which so often went with the name of magic.

We can read *Dr. Faustus* now only with a willing suspension, to the play's last syllable, of disbelief in magic. We can only read *The Tempest* now with a willing suspension of disbelief in magic; but, at its ending, magic has been emptied out of the world; it has served its poetic turn. It is indeed necessary to see *The Tempest* against the background of the long history of magical beliefs and of their tortuous relationships with a religious gnosis, and then, in Renaissance times at least, with Christianity; but if we then contemplate *The Tempest* in relation to the great changes in human belief and sensibility taking place in the seventeenth century, we may properly see it as the end of these confused syncretisms.

> *But this rough magic*
> *I here abjure; and . . .*
> *. . . I'll break my staff,*
> *Bury it certain fadoms in the earth,*

And deeper than did ever plummet sound
I'll drown my book.

Sir Thomas Browne will say that not to believe in witchcraft is to be atheistical; and Glanvil, so cool and sceptical,
and so anxious to accommodate religious belief to the
spirit of the new age of the late years of the seventeenth
century, will demonstrate the truth of witchcraft in order
that religious faith may be strengthened. In the eighteenth
century itself, Swift will urge the Duchess of Osmond 'to
get a lad touched for the evil'; between the lines and
through the denunciations of Addison's paper on the
superstitions of the times, written in 1711, some half-
dozen years after Locke's death, we can discern the still
strong sense of outrageous possibilities; Partridge, a person
of some classical attainments, travelling to Coventry with
his master in the middle years of the century, heard and
was terrified by evil spirits. But it is still true that *The
Tempest* provides an ending to the history of magic and
the occult in western Europe. Shakespeare's transcendent
genius made him a maker and therefore a prophet of our
modernity. Mr. Latham has said that to the race of fairies
created by Shakespeare in *A Midsummer Night's Dream*
can be traced 'the change in reputation and appearance
which the fairies of tradition and folk belief sustained,
and the subsidence of the race from the position of real
and fearful spirits'.[1] Shakespeare, who shows throughout

[1] In his book *The Elizabethan Fairies*, Columbia, 1930, p. 176, Mr.
Latham does not seek to maintain this statement *simpliciter*: Shakespeare
could only give leading and impetus, by his fairy creations, to an
inevitable change.

his plays the greatest acquaintance with the fairy lore of his time, helps incalculably to humanize these fearful creatures and thereby carry them over into the world of fancy. *Macbeth* could not have been written without a powerful imagination of supernatural evil; daemonic powers move here in our imaginations, not in our fancies; but it is also true that the superhuman in the play is so related to Macbeth's mind and heart that it comes to us as an extension, not a violation, of the human. In *A Midsummer Night's Dream* the daemonic is turned over to fancy; in *Macbeth* it is just kept within the imagination's vision of the world; in *The Tempest* we see the magical able still to serve the purpose of Shakespeare's profoundest imagination and thus belong to it and be identified with it; but we also see it as something which, in the end, the imagination must put an end to and have done with. Ariel is a daemon, or tetrarch, of the air; he is intelligible only in the light of the long history of European daemonology; but he is nearer to the fairy Puck than he and Puck are to the traditional daemons and fairies who had terrified men's minds over centuries of time. Ariel is too human to find a true place in the records of European daemonology; or, if we will, his creation marks a decisive moment in the concluding stages of these records. He had once been a servant of Sycorax and an instrument of her black Art. But he was too delicate a spirit for that, rebelled against her, and was imprisoned. Besides, if he rebelled against the black Art of Sycorax, he had no great love of Prospero's white magic either; and he will offer Prospero some lofty moral instruction. It is true enough that he is restless to be off; the island is indeed a prison to him; in the end the world of humanity bores him. This is all very well; but it is also true that the lineaments of his mind are all too human.

I am saying that when Prospero declares he will abjure his rough magic we behold his creator, the greatest spirit of our civilization, in these its early days, saying farewell to a whole region of the human imagination. There had been in Hellenistic times a sustained attempt to incorporate magic into a religious gnosis; and then in Renaissance times to reconcile it, at least in some of its forms, with Christianity. St. Augustine had made the position of the Church clear in the early years; and the Church was never to cherish illusions about magical beliefs and practices. But throughout these long centuries, the superhuman powers which magic sought to evoke were part of the Christian imagination also, whatever differences of interpretation there might be. This need not surprise us; magic could have its origin only in a religious imagination of the world; it is no primitive form of the scientific imagination. But now, in the writings of Shakespeare, we see the farewell of the human imagination to magic and all its ways, and to the hideous figures which had moved in it so long and to its inexpressible terror. Shakespeare is no doubt ahead of his age, as we should expect, and shaping its future.

7

It was not indeed only in the pages of the greatest imaginative artist of the age that we see the mind of

Europe discarding the image of a magical universe. In these years Sir Walter Raleigh was in the Tower of London, and writing his *History of the World*, which was to be published in 1614. What Raleigh has to say about magic in his pages illustrates also the climacteric to which the mind of Europe had come. Raleigh says that

the abuse of *Astrologie* did not terrifie *Abraham* . . . from observing the motions and natures of heavenly bodies; neither can it dehort wise and learned men in these daies from attributing those Vertues, influences, and inclinations to the Starres and other lights of heaven, which God hath given to those his glorious creatures. The sympatheticall and antipatheticall working of hearbes, plants, stones, minerals, with their other utmost vertues sometimes taught by the Deuill, and applied by his Ministers to harmful and uncharitable endes can never terrifie the honest and learned *Physician* or *Magician* from the using them to the helpe and comfort of mankinde. . . .

This is the envisagement of a Ficinian universe: there is no daemonic magic here; it is the astral magic which Raleigh allows for a part of the intellectual and spiritual life. But Raleigh is in truth looking away in his pages[1] from anything that can properly be called magic to 'natural philosophy', from the Renaissance magus to the modern scientist. So was Bacon, in whose pages there is no truck with magic in any form. Raleigh, indeed, with Hariot at his side, probably had clearer ideas about the nature and methods of science than Bacon had. Still, in Bacon's pages, as in Raleigh's, we see the prophecy of the

[1] *History of the World*, London, 1614, pp. 199–208.

huge coming of 'naturall philosophy', and of all the power, in contrast to the delusory 'powers' of the magician, which it was to bring with it for mankind.

For the Gray's Inn Revels of 1594,[1] Bacon wrote the addresses to the Mock-Prince of Purpoole. The address of the second Counsellor urges upon the Prince the 'study of philosophy'. 'Antiquity, that presenteth unto us dark Visions, the Wisdom of former Times, informeth us, that the Kingdoms have always had an Affinity with the Secrets and Mysteries of Learning. Amongst the PERSIANS, the Kings were attended on by the Magi . . . and generally those Kingdoms were accounted most happy, that had Rulers most addicted to philosophy. . . .' The Counsellor goes on to make specific recommendations. There were four. The last of them was that there be erected

a Still-House so furnished with Mills, Instruments, Furnaces and Vessels, as may be a Palace fit for a Philosophers Stone. Thus when your Excellency shall have added depth of knowledge to the fineness of Spirits and greatness of your Power, then indeed shall you be a TRISMEGISTUS; and then, when all other Miracles and Wonders shall cease, by reason that you shall have recovered their natural Causes, your self shall be left the only Miracle and Wonder of the World.[2]

All this anticipates the dedication of *The Advancement of Learning* to King James; and we see the figure of 'thrice-Great Hermes' being changed now into that of King

[1] For an account of the Revels, see Spedding, *Letters and Life*, vol. i, pp. 325–43, with its confident ascription of the Addresses to Bacon.

[2] *Gesta Grayorum*, London, 1688.

James. Bacon bows Trismegistus off the stage to bring in the Monarch in whose hands it lay to introduce the Kingdom of Man. Bacon and Shakespeare illustrate, in their different ways, the ending of an epoch. But King James as Bacon would have him, and Prospero as Shakespeare conceived *him*, are also worlds apart.

IV

THE NEW WORLD

I HAVE said enough to enable us to see Prospero the magician and Ariel his servant in relation to a long past of speculation and belief, to which, also, they provide a conclusion. I must now speak of Caliban. Caliban is primitive man as well as child of witch and devil; and it is necessary that I recount briefly the great events of the colonization of Virginia which form a major part of the background to Shakespeare's last play. I shall then return to the play's action.

I

It is probable that it was Englishmen who first, after the Norsemen, rediscovered North America: it seems that they had fished the Newfoundland Banks from 1490.[1] It was to be a long time before the English would settle in North America. But the writings of Amerigo Vespucci were to move powerfully in the mind of Sir Thomas More; they also inspired Thomas More's brother-in-law, John Rastell, to attempt to plant a colony in the northern part of the New World. More and Rastell were concerned with nothing less than colonization. The Utopians counted 'this the most just cause of war, when any people holdeth a piece of ground void and vacant, to

[1] D. B. Quinn, *The New Found Land*, Providence, 1965, pp. 7–8.

no good nor profitable use, keeping others from the use and possession of it'; and Rastell's concern was that Englishmen should make 'first building and habitation' in the northern part of the New World.[1] Cabot, sailing out from Bristol in 1497 and 1498 had confirmed a long coastline between Maine and Labrador: a sense of a new continent was dawning. In 1517 Rastell sailed from Greenwich, aided by the King. But his seamen would not face the Atlantic; they deserted, and abandoned Rastell in Ireland. Rastell was not to be the first to establish an English colony in America; but he was of the circle of the creator of Utopia. More forgot to ask Ralph Hythloday where Utopia was. Shakespeare was not to tell us where Prospero's island lay.

It was still to be a long time before Englishmen were to achieve any kind of settlement on the American continent. Far northern waters were principally to occupy their minds for many years. But in 1578 Sir Humphrey Gilbert 'switched his attention sharply and decisively to the temperate coasts of North America'.[2] The idea of an American settlement was growing; and the elder Hakluyt was already, in 1578, envisaging suitable sites for settlement in a temperate climate. What he wanted was a Mediterranean setting, 'in temperate Climat, in sweete ayre, where you may possesse alwayes sweete water, wood, seacoles, or turfe, with fish, flesh, grayne, fruits, herbes and rootes': a 'soyle and climate such as may yeelde you the Grape as good as that at Burdeus, as that

[1] See R. W. Chambers, *Thomas More*, New York, 1936, pp. 138–43.
[2] D. B. Quinn, *New Found Land*, p. 14.

in Portingale, or as that about Sivi [Seville] in Spaine, or that in the Ilands of the Canaries . . .'; and 'to plante upon an Ilande in the mouth of some notable river . . . were to great ende'.[1] Here was the elder Hakluyt's dream of an American–Mediterranean island conceived for the guidance of Sir Humphrey Gilbert. Roanoke and Jamestown were not far off now. The younger Hakluyt published these 'Notes on Colonisation' in 1582, in *Divers Voyages touching the Discovery of America*. Shakespeare was eighteen then.

Gilbert was lost in mid-Atlantic in September 1583. But in 1584 his half-brother, Walter Raleigh, took up the adventure of finding the island of the elder Hakluyt's dream. Gilbert had taken a northern route; Raleigh's men took Columbus's route, sailed up from the West Indies to Carolina and the islands and sand-bars which were ranged along its coast. The English colonization of North America was now to begin, and 'Virginia' discovered and named.

The two ships found a passage through the Carolina Banks below Roanoke Island. The two captains, Amadas and Barlowe, took formal possession of the island of Wococon in the Queen's name, quickly made contact with the Indians, crossed to Roanoke, and visited the home of the local chief in the north-west corner of the island. They were received there with the greatest kindness. They had made a first landing on 13 July 1584; by

[1] D. B. Quinn, *Voyages and Colonising Enterprises of Sir Humphrey Gilbert*, London, 1940, vol. i, pp. 181–5. Hakluyt the Preacher printed these notes of the Lawyer in his *Divers Voyages* of 1582.

mid-September they were home again, their recon-
naissance completed.

Arthur Barlowe, one of the captains, wrote an account
of the voyage for Raleigh. Hakluyt was to publish it in
the *Principall Navigations* in 1589; but it had been in
circulation in manuscript in 1584–5, and Holinshed
included a brief account of the journey in his *Chronicles* in
1587. It needs to be remembered that Barlowe's narrative
was in part intended to encourage later expeditions; and
it is possible that Hakluyt, in preparing it for the 1589
Principall Navigations removed from it any unpleasant
features and incidents. But however that may be, it is, as
we have it, a document of prodigious interest. After they
had taken possession, they 'viewed', says Barlowe,

the lande about vs, being whereas we first landed, very sandie,
and lowe towards the water side, but so full of grapes, as the
very beating, and surge of the Sea ouer-flowed them, of
which we founde such plentie, as well there, as in all places
else, both on the sande, and on the greene soile on the hills, as
in the plaines, as well on euery little shrubbe, as also climing
towardes the toppes of the high Cedars, that I thinke in all the
world the like aboundance is not to be founde: and myself
having seen those partes of Europe that most abound, finde
such difference, as were incredible to be written.[1]

Of Roanoke itself, Barlowe wrote:

We were entertained with all loue, and kindnes, and with as
much bountie, after their manner, as they could possibly
deuise. Wee founde the people most gentle, louing and

[1] D. B. Quinn, *The Roanoke Voyages*, London, 1955, vol. i, pp. 94–95.

faithfull, void of all guile, and treason, and such as liued after the manner of the golden age. The earth bringeth forth all things in aboundance, as in the first creation, without toile or labour. . . .

Utopia had been discovered, and Hakluyt's dream realized.

We are not to think that Prospero's island came first to Shakespeare's mind when news of the Bermuda shipwreck of 1609 came to England; the New World was in men's minds in Shakespeare's lifetime as journeying to the moon is in ours; and the journeys to America were more exciting (and, it seems, more dangerous) than ours to a fruitless moon. Another expedition, led by Sir Richard Grenville, a cousin of Raleigh's, sailed out from Plymouth for Virginia in April 1585. This time five ships and two pinnaces made the journey. The elder Hakluyt, in a note he wrote for Raleigh's guidance in planning the expedition, wrote: 'If we finde the countrey populous, and desirous to expel us, and iniuriously to offend us, that seeke but just and lawfull trafficke, then by reason that we are lords of navigation, and they not so, we are the better able to defend our selves by reason of those great rivers, and to annoy them in many places.'[1] More's justifiable war looked now like becoming a grim reality. Besides, earlier, in 1582, the younger Hakluyt, in his preface to *Divers Voyages* had written:

And surely if there were in us that desire to advance the honour of our Countrie which ought to bee in every good man, we

[1] E. G. R. Taylor, *Writings and Correspondence of the two Richard Hakluyts*, London, 1935, p. 329.

would not all this while have foreslown the possessing of those landes, which of equitie and right appertain unto us. . . . Yea, if we woulde beholde with the eye of pitie how al our prisons are pestered and filled with able men to serve their Countrie, which for smal robberies are dayly hanged up in great numbers, some twentie at a clappe out of one jayle (as was seene at the last assises at Rochester) wee woulde hasten and further every man to his power the deducting of some Colonies of our superfluous people unto those temperate and fertile parts of America, which being within six weekes sayling of England are yet unpossessed by any Christians: and seem to offer themselves unto us, stretching neerer unto her Majesties Dominions, then to any other part of Europe.[1]

Hakluyt was a humane man; but we can foresee that there will be Stephanos and Trinculos enough in Virginia in the years to come.

The first colony was now to be established. Grenville and his ships came to Wococon, as the ships of Amadas and Barlowe had done. Then there was shipwreck. Grenville's own ship, *Tyger*, struck and was nearly lost, and the priceless food in her went sour. It was an ill omen. When an expedition was made to the mainland, a dispute with the Indians broke out, and the Englishmen destroyed the corn and burnt the houses of an Indian village. The sweetness of the first meetings, in 1584, of Englishmen and Indians was at an end. The love of Prospero and Caliban for each other was to come to an end, too.

When Grenville left for home at the end of August, he left Ralph Lane in charge of the colony now established

---

[1] Ibid., pp. 175–6.

at Roanoke. Early in September, Lane wrote to Hakluyt, and said that if Virginia

had but horses and kine in some reasonable proportion, I dare assure my selfe being inhabited with Englishe, no realme in Christendome were comparable to it. For this already we finde, that what commodities soever Spaine, France, Italy, or the East partes doe yeeld unto us, in wines of all sortes, in oyles, in flaxe, in rosens, pitch, frankensence, corrans, sugers, and such like, these partes doe abound with the growth of them all, but being Savages that possesse the land, they know no use of the same. And sundry other rich commodities that no parts of the world, be they West or East Indies, have, here wee finde great abundance of.[1]

It seemed to be everything the elder Hakluyt dreamed of. But autumn and winter brought anxieties and hardship; and in the spring food ran short and bitterness between the English and the Indians sprang up. Suspicion and treachery grew, and 'plot was met with counterplot, and treachery with treachery. . . . Certainly, many illusions had been shattered on both sides. The settlers had been accepted as temporary God-like creatures in 1585; by 1586 they had become men who threatened the security of the Indian society and aroused savage cupidity by their wealth.'[2] Roanoke and Virginia were neither El Dorado nor Utopia. Grenville was to return in the spring with fresh supplies. He did not come. When, at last, in August,

[1] Hakluyt's *Principall Navigations, Voyages*, etc., Glasgow, 1904, vol. viii, p. 319.
[2] D. B. Quinn, *Raleigh and the British Empire*, New York, 1945, pp. 91–96.

he came, and with abundant supplies, the colonists were gone. They had seized a chance of going home with Drake. They had gone only a few days before a ship of Raleigh's arrived, and a fortnight before Grenville.

Ralph Lane wrote his account of this first colony of Englishmen in the New World. But there are two other memorials of it. Raleigh, under guidance from Hakluyt, had so thoughtfully planned his expedition, that there went with it a scientist and an artist. The scientist was Thomas Hariot; the artist, John White, who was also the expedition's cartographer. Of the earlier career of White we know little. We know a great deal about Hariot. He had been recommended to Raleigh about 1580, by, it seems, Raleigh's tutor at Oxford. He taught Raleigh 'the mathematicall sciences', and was to make contributions of the highest importance to the study of algebra, astronomy, and navigation. He was, Hakluyt was to say, 'to link theory with practice, not without almost incredible results'. But he was also to study the native Indians.[1] When Amadis and Barlowe came back, from the 1584 expedition, they brought with them two Indians, Manteo and Manchese. Hariot taught them English, learnt something of their language, learnt from them about their land and people: he thus prepared himself for his great tasks of observation and study on the Grenville expedition. Besides, everything that we learn about him leads us to see him as a man of rare quality and integrity. When he returned from the 1585 expedition he wrote a *Briefe and True Report of the New Found Land of Virginia*.

[1] D. B. Quinn, *Roanoke Voyages*, p. 37.

It was published in a beautifully printed Quarto in the very year of the Armada; and it is one of the rarest books in the world: it offers, says Mr. Craven, 'so fine an example of the printer's art and holds such historical significance that collectors of Americana regard it with a reverence comparable to that reserved by others for a Shakespeare Folio'.[1] Hakluyt printed it in his *Principall Navigations* in 1589. It is very likely that Shakespeare read it, either in the Quarto, or in Hakluyt. The first play in the Folio was to be in the debt of Hariot's Quarto. To this I shall return.

John White's water colours are hardly less priceless. They depict Indian figures, customs, and manners, and the natural history of the land. I quote Mr. Craven again: 'for skill in portraiture and interest of subject matter there is nothing comparable to these paintings of American life of earlier date than the eighteenth century'. Hakluyt was determined to give them, along with Hariot's *Briefe and True Report*, a wide circulation. Theodor de Bry met Hakluyt, Hariot, and White in London late in 1588 or early in 1589. In 1590 De Bry brought out Hariot's *Report* in Frankfurt, along with engravings of White's pictures and maps. The book (which is also of great beauty) appeared in four languages, English, Latin, French, and German; and between 1590 and 1620 it went through seventeen printings. The pictures De Bry chose for engraving were chiefly of the natives and of native life and manners. It seems indeed a far cry from the

[1] W. F. Craven, *The Southern Colonies in the Seventeenth Century*, Louisiana, 1949, p. 51

splendid Indian figures shown in White's paintings to
Caliban as he is ordinarily imagined and presented: but
we need to remember that it is hardly possible that Shakespeare did not see De Bry's engravings and that they were
not in his mind when he created Caliban. Here were the
first pictures, of extraordinary accuracy and beauty, of
the inhabitants of the New World; and we need to take
account of them in reading *The Tempest*, son of witch and
incubus as Caliban was.

If Shakespeare did not read Hariot's *Briefe and True
Report* in the Quarto of 1588 or in Hakluyt's *Principall
Navigations* of 1589, he will have read it in De Bry's book.
Besides, there were other books, preceding Hariot's, some
of which went, we may believe, to the making of *The
Tempest*. In 1582 Hakluyt himself brought out his
Divers Voyages; and during his time as Embassy chaplain
in Paris he had busied himself with arranging the publi-
cation of books concerning French and Spanish voyages
to the New World. He persuaded his friend Martin
Basanier to bring out, in 1586, in Paris, Laudonnière's
History of Florida, to which Hakluyt wrote a preface in
praise of Raleigh; and the 1589 *Principall Navigations*
contains an English translation of the book by Hakluyt.
In the summer of 1586 it became known in London that
the expedition of 1585–6 had failed. But Raleigh and
Hakluyt were not to be stopped, and another expedition
was to go out in 1587. Hakluyt persuaded Basanier to
bring out a French edition of Antonio Espejo's narrative
of his recent visit to New Mexico; and there followed
Hakluyt's complete edition of Pietro Martire Anghiera's

De Orbe Novo Decades, of which the first three 'decades' had been translated by Richard Eden, the Hakluyt of the mid-century, and published in 1555. In addition, there was brought out, in 1577, by Richard Willes, *The History of Travayle in the East and West Indies*, using, and adding to, the work done by Eden, who had died in 1576. Scholars have given good reason for thinking that Shakespeare was acquainted with the three 'Decades' of Peter Martyr which Eden had translated and with the *History of Travayle*; if their view is correct, as I believe it to be,[1] it is clear that Shakespeare read extensively in the literature of discovery. Shakespeare may have known little or nothing about the New World when he came to London; but he must have found it the talk of the town when he got there. Hakluyt's great book was published in 1589; and in the last years of the century Hakluyt had given to it, from his rectory in Wetheringsett, its final form. An immense literature of travel was at Shakespeare's disposal from 1589 onwards; and it would be eccentric to suppose that Shakespeare did all his reading of the literature of discovery immediately before he wrote *The Tempest*.

It is not to my purpose to relate at any length the fortunes of the expedition made in 1587. I wished especially to speak of the 1585 venture both because of its historic interest and because of the records of the New World provided by Hariot and White. Of the 1587 venture there

[1] The narrative in which the 'great deuill Setebos' occurs is included in both Eden's and Willes's books. Willes also included in his book Eden's translation of Peter Martyr's first three 'Decades'.

is, in any case, little enough to say: the men and women who embarked on it are lost to history. They may have been killed by Indians; they may have been absorbed by an Indian tribe; they may have taken to the ocean in a desperate hope. John White, the colony's Governor, had gone back early to secure help. There was tragic delay; and when he came to Roanoke in 1590 there was nothing of the colony to be seen; his own daughter and grand-daughter, Eleanor and Virginia Dare, were amongst the lost. The settlers had indeed gone to Roanoke; we know, however, that they were resolved to strike inland. But it was the 1607 expedition which was to found Jamestown.

The continuing war with Spain was now greatly to diminish, for the time being, if not to destroy, the chances of further colonization, to say nothing of reliev-ing the 'lost colony'. But Hariot's *Briefe and True Report* was made public in 1588; and, in the nineties, Hakluyt will complete his great work. Then, with the war over in 1604, there will be a new beginning in Virginia. The Preacher had been carefully listened to.

2

The first Virginia Charter was issued on 10 April 1606. The year before had probably seen the writing of *King Lear* and 1606, it seems likely, saw the writing of *Macbeth*: Shakespeare was at the height of his powers as a tragic dramatist. Colonization was now to begin on a new scale: the expeditions of the eighties of the previous century had gone ahead with the unofficial encouragement and

help of the Queen; the new ventures of the seventeenth
century went ahead under the declared authority of the
King and of a royal Charter. There were to be two ventures: one in the south, the other in the north, of 'Virginia'.
There was to be a royal Council of thirteen members,
sitting in London; and within each colony there was to be,
also, a governing body, of thirteen members. The action
of authority from the King to his London Council and
thence to a Council of Adventurers over the ocean was
bound to suffer impediments and difficulties: the authority
of the King in London was one thing; to establish and
maintain authority thousands of miles away was another.
Some of the colonists, and some of the royal councillors,
might reasonably be disposed to envisage a 'state of
nature' in the New World, with the 'earth bringing forth
all things in aboundance, as in the first creation, without
toile or labour', as Barlowe said; 'no name of magistrate,
no riches, poverty or use of service, none, no sovereignty',
as Gonzalo said;

> *Nature should bring forth,*
> *Of its own kind, all foison, all abundance,*
> *To feed my innocent people.*[1]

But in truth, in the face of physical difficulties, outrageous
conduct, and contumacy of all kinds, strong authority,
over Englishmen and Indians, there had to be: they
learnt this in bitterness and suffering. The younger
Hakluyt indeed, his feet ever firm on the ground, foresaw,
in 1584, in his celebrated *Discourse of Western Planting*,

---

[1] But no doubt Shakespeare had read Montaigne's essay, *Of Cannibals*.

something of the difficulties to come. In a chapter he probably added[1] to his *Discourse* after the return of Amadas and Barlowe, in 1584, he listed the food, articles, and tradesmen necessary for the next expedition; he went on to urge the manufacture and sale of knitted woollen caps 'to be prepared in London, Hereford, and Rosse'—he was from the borderland and was looking after his own— 'and to be vented to the people, and may be a notable trade of gaine to the marchaunte, and a great reliefe to oure poore people . . .'; then he goes on in his next paragraph to urge 'that there be appointed one or twoo preachers for the voyadge that God may be honoured, the people instructed, mutinies the better avoided, and obedience the better used, that the voyadge may have the better successe'.[2] There would be need of spiritual authority, and government and religion would be, if the Preacher had his way, no separate things. (They were not, indeed, to be separate things in the New World: we may think of John Winthrop and Roger Williams later in Massachusetts and Rhode Island; we may think, too, of Prospero, the priestly ruler of his colony, and dealing with as mixed a lot as Gates, De la Warr, and Winthrop had need to cope with.)

Late in 1606 some hundred men set sail for Virginia under the command of Christopher Newport. (They were chiefly artisans and labourers. But there were some gentlemen amongst them, and of these, too many were to wish to be leaders.) They reached Chesapeake Bay in

[1] D. B. Quinn, *Roanoke Voyages*, p. 18.
[2] E. G. R. Taylor, *Writings and Correspondence*, p. 324.

April 1607. They were to go inland, and seek a 'first seate' which would be better than Roanoke. They made their way about thirty miles up the James River, chose their spot, and called it Jamestown. But bitter disaffection broke out, and anger, and suspicion; it was no state of nature they came to; and the preacher, the Reverend Robert Hunt, an admirable man in an impossible role, failed to 'instruct the people' so as to 'avoid mutiny' or 'ensure obedience'.

The colonists had received from the London Council instructions to observe 'all just, kind and charitable courses' in their dealings with the Indians, under severe pains and penalties to be fixed by the Council of the colony. The official policy was not to dispossess the natives; it was to 'share with him the resources of a rich country and to confer upon him the benefit of a better life'.[1] Hakluyt the lawyer had written, as far back as 1585, that it should be carefully considered 'by what meane the people of those parties may be drawen by all courtesie into love with our nation; that we become not hatefull unto them, as the Spaniard is in Italie and in the West Indies, and elsewhere, by their maner of usage: for a gentle course without crueltie and tyrannie best answereth the profession of a Christian, best planteth the Christian religion';[2] and this remained the temper of the Council in London. But it was not easy. The Indian tribes were grouped into a confederacy led by a chief, Powhatan, who was quick, cautious, placatory, and treacher-

---

[1] W. F. Craven, op. cit., pp. 76–78.
[2] E. G. R. Taylor, op. cit., p. 334.

ous in his dealings with the English. The King's Council forbade violence towards him; and they resorted to an order requiring Powhatan to be crowned King, and to be given a palace of European design, in the hope, no doubt, that he would become a Christian. A copper crown was sent from England; and the celebrated Captain John Smith, now the head of the colony, and Christopher Newport enacted this pathetic and dubious ceremony. 'This island's mine, which thou tak'st from me . . . which first was mine own king', said Caliban; the English made Powhatan a king. But Powhatan could hardly be taken in by it, refused to kneel at the ceremony, and continued in his devious ways. Therefore, when in 1608 the great expedition of 1609 was being got ready, the Council in London agreed that Powhatan's influence must be overcome: no policy of ruthlessness was to be resorted to; still, all the tribes were to be directly tributary to the English.

It was indeed high time to reinforce the colony. However great the disappointment it had brought, much had been learnt, and a fairly firm foothold obtained. Schemes were evolved for development on an unprecedented scale, and joint stock finance resorted to. An appeal for subscribers resounded through London. Broadsides and pamphlets were issued. Sermons were preached to wish 'a good speed' to Virginia. Hakluyt and Hariot gave advice and counsel to the campaign; and Hakluyt both translated a Spanish book about Florida and arranged the translation of a French book about New France. It was little wonder that the appeal was successful in obtaining money and men. A new Charter was drawn up which made the Company virtually autonomous; and in future the colony was to have a governor whose powers were, under the Council in London, virtually absolute. Lord De la Warr was to be the first governor. In the end he could not go in 1609, and Sir Thomas Gates, a member of the Council, was to act in his place for the time being. Sir George Somers was to be Admiral of the Fleet, Christopher Newport its Vice-Admiral; and there was also William Strachey, who was to be appointed Secretary to the Council in Virginia. All four travelled in the same ship—the *Sea Adventure*—which on 15 May dropped down the Thames, and then on 2 June led out from Plymouth a fleet of nine vessels. No fleet of comparable size had ever set forth from England for the New World. There were some six hundred passengers—men and women.

3

In two years, it seems probable, Shakespeare will be writing *The Tempest*. No one will wish to exempt Shakespeare from the excitement of the events I have been describing. Besides, there is plenty of evidence that Shakespeare knew well a number of those deeply involved in, and responsible for, the great expedition of 1609. Mr. Gayley has set out the evidence,[1] and I need not repeat it here. Sir Edwin Sandys, Sir Henry Neville, Sir Fulk Greville were members of the 1607 Council; the

[1] In his book, *Shakespeare and the Founders of Liberty in America*, New York, 1917, chapter 2.

Earls of Pembroke and of Southampton, Christopher Brooke, Sir Dudley Digges, Lord Lisle, Lord De la Warr (to become Governor of Virginia in 1610), Sir Thomas Gates (appointed to act in De la Warr's place in 1609) were members of the reconstituted Council of 1609; the Earl of Montgomery, Pembroke's brother, became a member of the Council in 1612; Sir Henry Rainsford Shakespeare's neighbour at Clifford Chambers, near Stratford, became a member of the Council before Shakespeare died in 1616. Of all these men, we can say that Shakespeare either knew them or that his acquaintanceship with them was likely; and there were others: Donne (who would have liked to become Secretary of the Council in 1609 and became officially connected with the Company in 1622), Selden, who later became a member of the Council and one of its legal advisers, and Sir Henry Goodere of Polesworth in Warwickshire, a subscriber to the Company in 1611. There was also William Strachey. Another name I reserve for the moment.

It is necessary that I now speak briefly of Strachey. We cannot say with certainty that Shakespeare and Strachey were acquainted; we can only say that it is very probable. Until very recently, little was known about Strachey: we know a great deal more now thanks to the researches of Dr. Culliford.[1] We find Strachey, early in the new century, a friend of Ben Jonson's and a member of the Jonson circle. When *Sejanus* was first printed, in 1605, it was prefaced by verses by Chapman, Marston, Hugh Holland (who contributed a sonnet to Shakespeare's First Folio),

[1] S. G. Culliford, *William Strachey, 1572–1621*, Charlottesville, 1965.

a pseudonymous writer who was probably Richard Martin, a life-long friend of Strachey's, and by William Strachey himself. In general, it is certain that Strachey was well established in literary circles in the first decade of the century; he was also actively associated with the stage;[1] and *Sejanus* had first been acted by Shakespeare's Company at the Globe in 1603. It is difficult to think that Strachey and Shakespeare did not know each other, or indeed that they were no more than passing acquaintances.[2] Besides, their common interest in Virginia, to say nothing of their common literary and theatrical interests, must sooner or later have brought them together. When Strachey took with him to Virginia in 1609 copies of Acosta's *Naturall and Morale Historie of the East and West Indies* (which had been published in London in 1604), and of Willes's *History of Travayle*,[3] and very likely a copy of Hakluyt too, he took books which we may well believe Shakespeare had read and discussed with him. No doubt, too, he will have carried across the Atlantic, in his head if not in his baggage, Hariot's *Briefe and True Report*. Prospero's books were not the only ones to cross perilous seas.

When therefore the fleet set out from London for the New World in May 1609, there were on board the *Sea Adventure* Sir Thomas Gates, the expedition's leader, and William Strachey, who was to become Secretary to the

[1] Culliford, op. cit., pp. 52–55.

[2] In his introduction to the New Arden edition of *King Lear*, Mr. Muir gives reason for thinking that Strachey's sonnet written for *Sejanus* was in the debt of *King Lear*, which he thinks was partly written at the time of the publication of *Sejanus*.

[3] Culliford, op. cit., pp. 165–71.

Colony: both of them, in great probability, acquaintances, if not friends, of Shakespeare's. What happened is well known. The fleet took a more directly westerly course than earlier fleets had done: they wished to avoid Spanish waters. For seven weeks they sailed uneventfully, and were nearing Virginia. Then came a hurricane. For three days and four nights the storm drove the ships before it: 'The Sea swelled above the Clouds, and gave battell unto Heaven. It could not be said to rain, the waters like whole Rivers did flood in the ayre', Strachey was to write; 'nor a Starre by night, not Sunne beame by day was to be seene.' The *Sea Adventure* was separated from the other ships (which were to arrive safely in Virginia) and was driven to the Bermudas, 'the dangerous and dreaded Iland, or rather Ilands of the Bermuda . . . called commonly, The Devils Ilands';[1] she took in so much water that all (there were 150 passengers aboard) gave up hope. There was indeed no king on board; but at least Gates and Somers were King's representatives. The tempest ceased, and the ship was run in and wedged between two rocks. Nothing could save the *Sea Adventure*; but everyone got safely ashore, with their belongings, to find no devil's island, but a land of plentiful food, and a gentle winter. It was no wonder they thought it a divine deliverance. In the course of the winter they built two small vessels, and named them the *Patience* and the *Deliverance*. They made their way to Jamestown by May. That they should, after all, arrive seemed indeed miraculous—'by Providence divine'. But they found the colony

[1] *Purchas His Pilgrimes*, Glasgow, 1896, vol. xix, pp. 7–13.

in Jamestown in a disastrous condition. John Smith had kept the earlier colony in existence in the face of terrible difficulties which I need not here recount. The coming of the new colonists in 1609, some 400 of them, had made things a great deal worse: little, if any, provision had been made for them; there seemed every good reason to believe their Governor lost with the *Sea Adventure*: there was no authority. The winter proved terrible. Large numbers starved to death; only sixty were alive to greet Gates and Somers when they arrived in the *Patience* and the *Deliverance* in May of 1610. Exhausted by their journey, unprovided with shelter, ravaged by epidemics, demoralized and listless, they had not coped with the problems of the food supply. Above all, they had been leaderless; and there were too 'many unruly gallants packed thither by their friends to escape ill destinies: and those would dispose and determine of the government sometimes one way, the next day another, to day the old commission, to morrow the new, the next day by neither. In fine, they would rule all or ruine all.'[1] This is what the great expedition of 1609 had come to. It is not difficult to imagine the dismay with which the news of the colony, with Gates and Somers believed lost, was received in London in the autumn of 1609. It is harder to imagine the satisfaction and sneers of many at yet another improvident and unnecessary venture.

The Council in London entered for publication on

[1] *Works of Capt. John Smith*, ed. Edward Arber, London, 1895, vol. i, p. 162. The quotation here given is taken from a book compiled by W. Symonds from eyewitnesses, and published in Oxford in 1612.

14 December 1609 *A True and Sincere Declaration of the purpose and ends of the Plantation begun in Virginia.* No doubt it was published very soon after this date. The Council put out a Broadside[1] at about the same time. Shakespeare must have read them. The *True and Sincere Declaration* is a masterly, noble, and moving document, and was heavy with destiny for the future of England and the United States. Urgent with religious passion, it went over the reasons for the establishment of the colony, justified the route the fleet had taken (an experimental journey had been made over it), recounted what had happened to the fleet, and announced the Council's resolve to send Lord De la Warr (who was, in any case, Governor-elect) to lead another expedition. The document is full of resolution:

that which seems to disharten or shake our first grounds in this supply; ariseth from two principal sources, of which one was the cause of the other; First, the Tempest: and can any man expect an answer for that? Next the *absence* of the Governor, an effect of the former, for the loss of him is in suspence, and much reason of his safety against some doubt; and the hand of God reacheth all the Earth. . . . If we consider I say and compare these certainties and truths, as less ends to strengthen and produce our first and principal, with those casual and accidental misadventures and errors, which have befallen us, before every equal and resolved heart, they will vanish and become smoke and air, and not only keep upright but raise

[1] The *Declaration* and the Broadside can be read in Alexander Brown, *The Genesis of the United States*, Boston, 1890, vol. i, pp. 338–56, whence the following quotations are taken.

our spirits and affections, and reconcile our reasons to our desires.

The *Declaration* ends with an impassioned appeal 'so to nourish this graine of seed, that it may spread till all the people of the earth admire the greatnesse and seeke the shades and fruite thereof'. These were, indeed, to prove prophetic words.

One other thing the *Declaration* and the Broadside made clear: there would be careful choice of those who would sail with De la Warr; 'for that former experience hath too dearely taught, how much and manie ways it hurteth to suffer Parents to disburden themselves of lascivious sonnes, masters of bad servants and wives of ill husbands, and so to clogge the businesse with such an idle crue, as did thrust themselves in the last voiage, that will rather starve for hunger, than lay their hands to labor.'

It was spring before De la Warr left, with three ships and 150 men. There had been delay in his getting away. But on 21 February William Crashaw (the father of the poet) preached before Lord De la Warr, and others of the King's Virginia Council, to mark De la Warr's impending departure. The sermon was entered at Stationers' Hall on 19 March and given the title 'a Newe yeres Gifte to Virginia'. The sermon, one of great eloquence and power, needs to be read in order to realize the depth of feeling about the New World which animated the Church of England at the time. It is bitterly anti-papistical and anti-separatist (the Pilgrim Fathers were to sail in ten years' time), and is filled with a sense of the missionary duty of the English Church towards the New World. Crashaw spoke of the enemies of the Virginia colony. There were three. The first was the Devil. The second was the Papists. The third was the Players. Shakespeare may have sat in a congregation composed of members of the Council and other persons interested in the future of Virginia; or, if not he may well have read the sermon when it was published in March. If he did so, he will have taken amused notice of these worlds of Crashaw's:

As for the Plaiers: (pardon me right Honourable and beloved, for wronging this place and your patience with so base a subject,), they play with Princes and Potentates, Magistrates and Ministers, nay with God, Religion, and all holy things: nothing that is good, excellent or holy can escape them: how then can this action? But this may suffice, that they are but Players: they abuse Virginea, but they are but Players; they disgrace it: true, but they are but Players, and they have played with better things, and such as for which, if they speedily repent not, I dare say Vengeance waites for them.[1]

Perhaps now, early in 1610, the idea of writing a play in which the New World would appear was beginning to stir in Shakespeare's mind; or perhaps it was Crashaw's sermon that put the idea vaguely in his head; in any case, he would have to watch his step.

De la Warr reached Virginia in early June. He was just in time. Those of the colony who had survived were on their way down the James River to make for home when De la Warr sent news of his arrival at the mouth of the river. Somers, who, to judge by Silvester Jourdain's account, had been a masterful leader of those on the *Sea*

[1] Brown, *Genesis of the United States*, pp. 366-7.

Adventure, went off to Bermuda to obtain food. But he did
not come back: he died in Bermuda. In the face of a desperate situation, Sir Thomas Gates sailed for England and
reached there in September, and his news must have been
received with hardly bearable credulity. Jourdain, who
had been on the *Sea Adventure*, came home with Gates, and
promptly put out, in October, his *Discovery of the Barmudas*:
Shakespeare will surely have read his account of the storm,
of islands 'ever esteemed, and reputed, a most prodigious
and inchanted place', which proved a place of salvation,
of Somers's courage and masterfulness, and of the journey
to Jamestown. Gates left the Virginia Council in no doubt
of the plight of the colony; nor indeed of the prospect,
in spite of everything, of the great wealth to be found
in Virginia. The Council rose once more to the occasion, put out in November *A True Declaration of the estate
of the Colonie in Virginia, With a confutation of such scan-
dalous reports as have tended to the disgrace of so worthy an enter-
prise*, and raised eighteen thousand pounds by the spring.

A True Declaration is a more extensive document than
its predecessor, *A True and Sincere Declaration*,[1] which had
been published in December 1609. The case needed now
to be set out yet more urgently and fully; and in any case
there was more to say: there had been a clear interven-
tion of Providence. Like its Predecessor, it is a masterpiece of rhetorical prose. I do not now propose to
resume its argument; and those features of it which show

[1] Of the two *Declarations*, the second is to be found in Peter Force's
Tracts, vol. 3; Washington, 1844; the first, with the Broadside, in
Brown, *Genesis of the United States*, vol. i, pp. 337–56.

that it was running in Shakespeare's head when he was composing *The Tempest* have been observed by others:[1] I need not recount them here. I will only say that *A True Declaration* requires to be read as a document which, in its ordering of fact and argument, and in its majestic eloquence, exceeds only *A True and Sincere Declaration* in communicating to us the feel and pressure of the time in its resolve to create a new English world and a vast extension of the Kingdom of Man.

4

The Kingdom of Man! The phrase is Francis Bacon's, who in the *New Atlantis* was to speak of 'enlarging the bounds of human empire'. To whom did the Virginia Council turn to compose the *Declarations*, so critical for the future of civilization in the West? We need to remember that the meetings of the Council were held in secrecy. To whom, of their number, would they turn? I do not doubt that it was to the Solicitor-General, incomparably the greatest advocate and orator of the age. The writer of *A True Declaration* 'professeth that he will relate nothing (concerning *Virginia*) but what he hath from the secrets of the iudiciall councell of *Virginia* from the letters of Lord *La Ware*, from the mouth of *Sir Thomas Gates*, whose wisdomes (he conceiueth) are not so shallow, as easily to be deceiued of *others* nor consciences

---

[1] By Mr. R. R. Cawley in *P.M.L.A.*, vol. xli, 1926. See also Mr. Kermode's Arden edition, p. xxix. I add that a phrase used in the *True Declaration*—'the tempest of dissention'—may well have stuck in Shakespeare's mind.

so wretched, as by pretences to deceiue others'. He was clearly a person of great position and authority; and he does not hesitate to use the first person singular: nor had the writer of *A True and Sincere Declaration*.

Bacon became a member of the reconstituted Council in the first half of 1609. He, like so many of those names I have given above of men known to Shakespeare— Southampton, Sir Henry Neville, Lord De la Warr, to mention three who had taken part in the Essex rising of 1601—had been an Essex man—for a time; he, with Sir Henry Hobart, drew up the second and third Virginia Charters, and very likely aided Sir Edwin Sandys, with whom he was closely associated at this time in the drafting of a number of matters, in drawing up the first draft of the second.[1] And there is no need for me to recount here the evidence of Bacon's impassioned interest in colonization, in Virginia and elsewhere.

Bacon's authorship of the *Declarations*, or, at the least, his great hand in their composition, becomes clear to anyone who, having read over the *Declarations*, recalls, or then reads over, others of Bacon's writings. To read over the first book of *The Advancement of Learning* is to see the same style, ordonnance, and learning at work as show themselves in the *Declarations*; or again, there are *Of the True Greatness of the Kingdom of Britain* (1608), and *An Advertisement touching an Holy War* (1622); there are also, smaller in scope, the essays *Of the True Greatness of Kingdoms and Estates* and *Of Plantations*. The same hand is to be seen in all.

[1] Brown, *Genesis of the United States*, vol. i, pp. vii and 207.

The reader of the two *Declarations* will see that the first is plainer, more direct, and less learned than the second; it is in the second that Bacon exercises his full armoury, both in its depth or argumentation and in its manner: it is full of Bacon's magnanimity, and that 'high learning, which he wore with as little concealment as a diamond'.[1] But in the first are the words which I quoted earlier from the prayer with which *A True and Sincere Declaration* ends, where we read of the 'nourishing' of the 'graine of seed, that it may spread till all the people of the earth admire the greatnesse, and seeke the shades and fruite thereof'. This image recurs, again and again, in the writings to which I have just referred. In *Of the True Greatness of the Kingdom of Britain*, written, it seems, in 1608, we read that 'the true greatness of kingdoms upon earth is not without some analogy with the kingdom of Heaven, as our Saviour describes it: which he doth resemble not to any great *kernel* or *nut*, but to one of the least *grains*, but yet such a one as hath a property to grow and spread'.[2] I will not here trouble the reader with other versions of this image which Bacon from time to time employed, except for one. On 23 February 1621 Bacon replied in Parliament to a speech of a newly appointed Speaker of the House of Commons. In the course of his speech, he said: 'This kingdom now first in his Majesty's times hath gotten a lot or portion in the New World, by the plantation of Virginia and the Summer Islands. And certainly it is with the kingdoms on earth as it is in the kingdom of heaven.

[1] David Mathew, *The Jacobean Age*, London, 1938, p. 144.
[2] *Works*, Spedding and Ellis, vol. xiii, p. 234.

Sometimes a grain of mustardseed proves a great tree. Who can tell?'[1]

Finally, I observe that, in the *True Declaration*, we read: 'and though it bee not for a theoreticall Scholar, to circumscribe the dominions of Princes, yet a few proofes from antiquity, shall suffice to controwle ignorant or presumptuous follie'. It seems strange to find Bacon, the Solicitor-General, speaking of himself as a 'theoreticall Scholar'. But in truth, Bacon greatly cherished this idea of himself. In writing to Villiers, the new favourite of the King, in 1616, Bacon wrote: 'You know I am no courtier, nor versed in state affairs. My life hitherto rather hath been contemplative than active. I have rather studied books than men.' How could Bacon speak like this— Solicitor-General in 1607, Attorney-General in 1613, soon to be Lord Keeper and Lord Chancellor? But he did so; and his calling himself, in the second *Declaration*, 'a theoreticall Scholar' comes not to throw doubt on Bacon's authorship of it, but to confirm it further.

Thus, in reading the *Declarations*, Shakespeare felt something of the impact of the man who in that time was alone comparable to him in greatness, profoundly as the quality, bent, and vision of their minds differed. They both gave their renderings of the tempest[2] of 1609. It was Bacon who

---

[1] Spedding, *Letters and Life*, vol. 7, p. 175.

[2] Archbishop Tenison, in his *Baconiana Or Certain Genuine Remains of Sir Francis Bacon*, published in London in 1679, wrote of the 'severities' which Bacon suffered during and after his fall, that they 'proved, by accident, happy Crosses and Misfortunes'. 'Methinks', he went on, 'they are resembled by those of Sir *George Sommers*, who being bound, by his Employment, to another Coast, was by Tempest cast upon the *Bar-*

had said that Englishmen ought 'so to nourish this graine of seed, that it may spread till all the people of the earth admire the greatnesse and seeke the shades and fruit thereof'. In saying this, Bacon was indeed prophetic, as he was of other mighty things. Shakespeare's play was to be prophetic, too; it was also to be a play of sober disillusion: Miranda's brave new world was not the real world.

5

It is necessary now to turn again to William Strachey before looking again to the play and to the figure of Caliban. Strachey had gone off in the *Sea Adventure* to try his fortunes; but having come, in the end, to Virginia, he was appointed Secretary to the Colony and occupied a key place in its life and affairs from the time he arrived in Jamestown with Gates and Somers in May 1610 until he left for home in the autumn of 1611. Having arrived in Jamestown, and seen the desperate state of affairs there, he composed a letter, for a lady whose name we do not know, describing the journey of the *Sea Adventure*, their 'redemption', the winter in Bermuda, contumacy and mutiny there, and conspiracy to murder the Governor, Sir Thomas Gates, their journey to Jamestown, and what

mudas. And there, a Shipwrack'd Man made full discovery of a new temperate fruitful Region, which none had before inhabited; and which Mariners, who had only seen its Rocks, had esteemed an inaccessible and enchanted place.' (Edition of 1679, p. 16.) It is strange that Tenison should thus speak of Bacon's last years. Had he perhaps a copy of *A True Declaration* amongst the papers? If he had a manuscript, it will not have been in Bacon's or Rawley's handwriting (see Tenison, p. 79).

they found there. This letter is ordinarily called *A true reportory of the wracke, and redemption of Sir Thomas Gates.*[1] Sir Thomas Gates brought it home with him, along with a formal report signed by De la Warr, Gates, and Strachey. Strachey's letter and the report were quickly in the hands of the Virginia Council in London, of which Gates was himself a member. Strachey's letter could not be published; he could hardly have hoped that it would be; it was too candid and shocking for that; but along with what Gates told the Council, it was to provide the material for *A True Declaration.* Strachey wrote vividly and with an eye for detail of many kinds; and *A Reportory of the wracke* stands as a notable piece of literature in itself, recording faithfully and with every sense of what was at stake a story of resolution, terror, relief, courage, hope, hope deferred, utter demoralization; all this, and more. I need not recount here the debts of *The Tempest* to Strachey's *Reportory.* They have frequently been observed. I remark now only that it is a matter of great interest that Shakespeare read (as he quite certainly did) this highly confidential letter—one of the 'secrets' of the Council; but this, because of his friends on the Council, need not surprise us.[2]

[1] It will be found in *Purchas His Pilgrimes*, Glasgow, 1906, vol. xix. But it now appears in an easily available and convenient form in Mr. Louis Wright's *A Voyage to Virginia*, Virginia, 1964. The volume also contains Jourdain's *Discovery of the Barmudas*.

[2] Looking at a copy, in the Beinecke Library of Yale, of Richard Willes's *History of Travayle* (1577), I saw on the title-page the signature of William Strachey. Beneath the signature, in the same handwriting was a date: *May 2, 1609.* On 15 May of that year the greater part of the

Strachey came back in the following year. When, in 1611, he arrived in England, we do not know for certain. *The Tempest* will be given one of its earliest performances, if not its very first, on 11 November 1611. It would therefore be of great interest to know if Strachey were back in time to discuss Virginia with Shakespeare before *The Tempest* took its final shape for performance later that year.[1]

As I have said, Strachey's letter could not be published, and Strachey will not have imagined that it could be. But his ambitions as a writer, together with his recent experiences as a voyager, prompted him to write a book of travel.[2] But this would take some time to prepare. In the meantime, he would bring out a collection of the laws for Virginia which had been framed by Sir Thomas Gates

fleet set sail for Virginia from London and was joined by two other ships at Plymouth before setting out. Dr. Culliford provides conclusive reasons for believing that Strachey had a copy of Willes's book at his elbow while composing the *Reportory* (*William Strachey*, pp. 167–71); and it therefore seems reasonable to assume that the Beinecke copy went off with Strachey in the *Sea Adventure*, suffered the tempest, was taken off at Bermuda, and carried in one of the pinnaces to Virginia. If this assumption is indeed justified, the Beinecke Library is to be congratulated on possessing a book of prodigious historic interest.

[1] It has been customary to say that Strachey probably arrived back in late October or early November; and this is Dr. Culliford's view also. He thinks that Strachey 'probably' left Virginia in the *Prosperous* which left Virginia in September. But I gather from a reference he gives, on p. 126, to Brown's *Genesis of the United States* that he thinks it possible that Strachey came home earlier, perhaps in the *Elizabeth*, which left Jamestown in July.

[2] Dr. Culliford (pp. 184–9 of *William Strachey*) advances good reason for believing that Strachey began his *Historie of Travell* in Virginia; he further thinks it possible that it was begun in Bermuda.

and expanded by his successors in the Governorship: Lord
De la Warr and Sir Thomas Dale. He wrote an introduction to his collection, and entered the volume for
publication in December 1611; it was published the
following month. The *True Reportory* shows how well
Strachey could write; his preface to the *Lawes* of Virginia
shows how badly he could write. But at least it makes
clear, in spite of all its verbiage, that he is preparing a
book which will recount his time in the Bermudas and in
Virginia; there were impediments, he said, which must
as yet 'detain' his observations 'in the shadow of dark-
nesse'.[1]

But the book was not published. He finished it, such as
it was, by the end of 1612; he then tried to hurry it into
print, when it clearly did not represent what, according
to his preface to the *Lawes*, he had set out to do. It is not,
alas, a narrative of his own experiences and in particular
of his time in Jamestown. It is largely a compilation of
accounts given by others.[2] But in one place Strachey
speaks of the Indians from his own experience and knowledge; and in this lies the chief value of his book. Even
here he draws on Hariot's *Briefe and True Report* as well as
on Captain John Smith's *Map of Virginia* which had been
published in 1612; still, what Strachey had to say in these
pages, out of his own observation, is of great importance.
I said that Hariot comes back into the picture: so does
John White. The Princeton MS., which Mr. Wright and

[1] Force's *Tracts*, vol. 3, p. (5) of *For the Colony in Virginea Brittannia*.
[2] Dr. Culliford speaks at length of Strachey's *Historie of Travell* in his
book, pp. 165–84.

Mrs. Freund used for their edition of Strachey's *Historie of Travell into Virginia Britannia*, has with it (as the other manuscripts have) twenty-seven engravings from De Bry's 1590 edition of Hariot's *Briefe and True Report*. I add only this, before turning to the Caliban of Shakespeare's play. Strachey's first manuscript of his book was dedicated to the Earl of Northumberland, to whom I have referred earlier, who was a generous patron of Hariot, and whose brother went to Virginia in 1606 and was acting governor there in 1609; a second manuscript was presented to Sir Allen Apsley, Purveror to the Navy, but again, it was not published; a third manuscript was presented to Bacon in 1618. Bacon was now Lord Verulam and Lord Chancellor. Strachey took his chance, and sent a manuscript of his work to Verulam, with a dedicatory letter of great interest.

Your Lordship ever approving yourself [wrote Strachey] a most notable fautor of the Virginian Plantation, being from the beginning (with other lords and earles) of the principall counsell applyed to propagate and quide yt: and my poore self (bound to your observaunce, by being one of the Graies-Inne Societe) having bene there three yeares thither imploied in place of secretarie so long there present; and setting downe with all my wel-meaning abilities a true narration or historie of the countrie: to whom shoulde I submitt so aptly, and with so much dutye, the most humble present thereof, as to your most worthie and best-judging Lordship? who in all vertuous and religious endeavours have ever bene, as a supreame encourager, so an inimitable patterne and perfecter: nor shall my plaine and rude composition any thought discourage my attempt, since howsoever I should feare to appeare therein before so matchles a maister in that facultie (if any opinionate worth of mine owne worke presented me) yet as the great Composer of all things made all good with his owne goodnes, and in our only will to his imitation takes us into his act, so be his goodnes your good Lordship's in this acceptation.[1]

Bacon did not reply. It was Strachey's last throw in his efforts to get his book published. He died in 1621.

6

I turn now to the figure of Caliban. I have said there was nothing unimaginable to a Jacobean audience in a creature born of witch and incubus. But I have also said that Shakespeare will have had in mind John White's drawings of the Indians he saw on Grenville's expedition of 1585. If Caliban emerges out of the murky past of daemonology and witchcraft, he also emerges as a human figure out of a New World whose inhabitants had been disclosed in White's drawings to the gaze of the ancient civilization of Europe. Shakespeare had taken on a complicated job. He must have his magician and his daemonology, and his Ariel; and Caliban must somehow belong to their world. But Prospero is also the Old World in its dealings with the New; and in this world, Caliban is no monster but a man; and nowhere in *The Tempest* is Caliban to be seen as less than human.[2] Caliban was

[1] R. H. Major in his edition of Strachey's *Historie of Travell*, London, 1849, used the 'Bacon' manuscript. The edition of Louis B. Wright and Virginia Freund, London, 1953, uses the 'Northumberland' manuscript.

[2] Mr. Kermode, in his Arden edition of *The Tempest* (p. 63), quotes Malone as saying that Caliban's dress, 'which doubtless was originally

'a freckled whelp hag-born', says Prospero; but in the next line he gives him 'a human shape'. Prospero indeed also calls him 'a mis-shapen knave', and says that he is 'as disproportion'd in his manners as in his shape'; but it is Trinculo, Stephano, and Antonio who talk of a monster and a fish. Prospero speaks vaguely of Caliban's mis-shapenness in describing a creature represented as of monstrous birth: some measure of compromise there had to be, in order to relate the 'poor Indian' to the offspring of witch and daemon.

But it is also true that Prospero everywhere pours scorn and loathing on Caliban: Caliban was 'filth', a 'demi-devil', 'capable of all ill', 'would take no print of goodness' and was a 'born slave' beyond the reach of freedom. There could, indeed, be no question of Shakespeare's giving a sentimental picture of the primitive Indian. No doubt he had read the early descriptions of the Indians by Hariot and Barlowe; but by 1610 the picture had changed. The author of the *True Declaration* spoke of the ills and accidents that befell the colony of 1609; and he went on to describe how Powhatan like 'a greedy vulture' carried out ambush and massacre at the expense of the enfeebled colony. This, or something like it, had become the picture of the Indian which now prevailed and was officially acknowledged; and there was nothing,

prescribed by the poet himself and has been confirmed since his time, is a large bear-skin, or the skin of some other animal; and he is usually represented with long shaggy hair'. This is in accordance with Hariot's 'They are a people clothed with loose mantles made of deere skinnes, and aprons of the same round about their middles, all els naked . . .' (Quinn's *Roanoke Voyages*, pp. 368–89).

in Prospero's eyes, which relieved the malignity of Caliban.

But Shakespeare is at pains to recount the history of Caliban from the time of Prospero's coming to the island, and it is clear that there is much more to Caliban than Prospero allows. Caliban's age, when Prospero came to the island, can, we may suppose, be measured by Ariel's twelve years' imprisonment; and Sycorax had died within the space of these twelve years, leaving the island

> *Save for the son that she did litter here,*
> *A freckled whelp hag-born—not honour'd with*
> *A human shape.*

But when Prospero came to the island Caliban was alone and languageless.[1]

> *When thou cam'st first, says Caliban,*
> *Thou strok'st me, and made much of me; would'st give me*
> *Water with berries in't; and teach me how*
> *To name the bigger light, and how the less,*
> *That burn by day and night; and then I lov'd thee,*
> *And show'd thee all the qualities o' th' isle,*
> *The fresh springs, brine-pits, barren place and fertile.*
> *Cursed be I that did so! . . . All the charms*
> *Of Sycorax: toads, beetles, bats, light on you!*
> *For I am all the subjects that you have,*

[1] It will be observed, in the extended quotation which follows, that Prospero speaks of providing to Caliban the power of speech; and Caliban says, 'You taught me language.' But later in the same speech, Caliban reproaches Prospero for teaching him '*your* language'.

Which first was mine own King: and here you sty me
In this hard rock, whiles you do keep from me
The rest o' th' island.

Prospero: *Thou most lying slave,*
Whom stripes may move, not kindness! I have us'd thee
Filth as thou art, with human care: and lodg'd thee
In mine own cell, till thou didst seek to violate
The honour of my child.

Caliban: *O ho, O ho! would't had been done!*
Thou didst prevent me; I had peopled else
This isle with Calibans.

Prospero: *Abhorred slave*
Which any print of goodness wilt not take,
Being capable of all ill! I pitied thee,
Took pains to make thee speak, taught thee each hour
One thing or other: when thou did'st not, savage,
Know thine own meaning, but would'st gabble like
A thing most brutish, I endow'd thy purposes
With words that made them known. But thy vile race,
Though thou did'st learn, had that in't which good natures
Could not abide to be with; therefore wast thou
Deservedly confined into this rock,
Who hadst deserv'd more than a prison.[1]

Caliban: *You taught me language; and my profit on't*
Is, I know how to curse. The red plague rid you
For learning me your language.

[1] This speech is given in the Folio to Miranda; and Professor Kermode follows the Folio. I can only say that I find it incredible that
Shakespeare intended this speech for Miranda, not Prospero.

And when Prospero orders him off to fetch his logs, Caliban says:

> *I must obey: his Art is of such pow'r*
> *It would control my dam's god, Setebos,*
> *And make a vassal of him.*

This, then, is the history of Caliban up to the time of the play's beginning; and I now comment briefly upon it before those coming straight from the sophistication of Naples and Milan appear upon the scene, and initiate the proper action of the play.

In the beginning, Prospero had cherished Caliban, and Caliban loved Prospero in return. But Caliban will be so quick at a later stage to take Stephano for a god that we may fairly assume that he had earlier taken Prospero for one. Thus the Indians in the early days had been disposed to view the white man. Prospero, like Stephano, must have dropped from heaven. 'Hast thou not dropped from heaven?' he said to Stephano; and when Stephano declares himself the man in the moon, Caliban says:

> *I have seen thee in her, and I do adore thee:*
> *My mistress show'd me thee, and thy dog, and thy bush.*

For Stephano, Caliban will do what he had done for Prospero when Prospero loved him:

> *I prithee, let me bring thee where crabs grow;*
> *And I with my long nails will dig thee pig-nuts;*
> *Show thee a jay's nest, and instruct thee how*
> *To snare the nimble marmoset: I'll bring thee*

> *To clustering filberts, and sometimes I'll get thee*
> *Young scamels from the rock. Wilt thou go with me?*

And then, if Caliban will speak like this, filled with the wonder of the world he sees and knows, he will also speak of the wonder of what transcends the world.

> *Be not afeard; the isle is full of noises,*
> *Sounds and sweet airs, that give delight, and hurt not.*
> *Sometimes a thousand twangling instruments*
> *Will hum about mine ears; and sometimes voices,*
> *That, if I then had wak'd after long sleep,*
> *Will make me sleep again: and then, in dreaming,*
> *The clouds methought would open, and show riches*
> *Ready to drop upon me; that, when I wak'd,*
> *I cried to dream again.*

What shall we say of this? There is first the music Caliban hears, and then the voices; and the voices win him back to sleep and dreams after long sleep; and then, in dream, the clouds open to him and show him riches ready to be yielded to him; but they are denied him by his waking; his waking is a morning; and he cries to dream again. Mr. Robert Graves has remarked that in these lines there is 'an illogical sequence of tenses which creates a perfect suspension of time'; and this is so. Caliban is not narrating his past, but describing his continuing condition: his continuing sense of wonder and mystery, and of a transcendent and supernatural life to which also the 'perfect suspension of time' applies. This is the dreaming innocence and grace of Caliban. At a later stage in the play, Prospero, in words as famous as those of Caliban, will speak of sleep and dream, and of our life in terms of them:

> *We are such stuff*
> *As dreams are made on; and our little life*
> *Is rounded with a sleep.*

I shall speak later of these last lines; but I remark now that if Caliban's lines disclose the deepest truth about him, what above all Shakespeare saw in the primitive man about whom such contradictory reports came to him from the New World, Prospero will yet say of him that he is a born devil, upon whose nature nurture will never stick, on whom all his pains had been quite lost. Prospero is the highest and most spiritual form of sophistication in the play; yet he can speak like this of Caliban. This is not all, indeed, as we shall see, that Prospero has to say about Caliban. But I shall now give, in what may seem a strange apposition to the lines of Caliban of which I have been speaking, these words from one of the greatest spirits of Christendom:

In this Divine union the soul sees and tastes abundance, inestimable riches, finds all the rest and the recreation that it desires, and understands strange kinds of knowledge and secrets of God, which is another of those kinds of food that it likes best. It feels likewise in God an awful power and strength which transcends all other power and strength: it tastes a marvellous sweetness and spiritual delight, finds true rest and Divine light and has lofty experience of the knowledge of God, which shines forth in the harmony of the creatures and the acts of

God. Likewise, it feels itself to be full of good things and far withdrawn from evil things and empty of them; and, above all, it experiences, and has fruition of, an inestimable feast of love. . . .

It may seem a far cry from Shakespeare's Caliban to the mysticism of St. John of the Cross. But in truth, it is not so far.[1] Shakespeare was writing within the limits imposed by the secular Jacobean theatre; and we see Caliban, in his primitiveness, credulity, polytheism, terrified by daemons and spirits (which he distinguishes from 'gods')[2] which set upon him; but he is also, in his helplessness and dependence, exposed to a mysterious and transcendent reality. This, in the end, is 'the thing itself', divided, in the encompassing darkness, between terror and love, despair and adoration, and aware, above all, of a transcendent, supernatural world. This is Caliban disclosing to us the primary fact about our life; and I add that if Shakespeare's play may be said to be *about* anything, it is, for one thing, about the tragic diminution, which 'sophistication' and

[1] 'The very dialectic of the sacred tends indefinitely to repeat a series of archetypes, so that a hierophany realized at a certain "historical moment" is structurally equivalent to a hierophany a thousand years earlier or later' (Mercia Eliade, *Shamanism*, New York, 1964, p. xvii). Not that there were a thousand years between the religion of Caliban and of St. John of the Cross. The statement from Hariot's *Report* which follows in the text was written during the lifetime of St. John of the Cross. (The quotation from St. John of the Cross is taken from Allison Peers's translation.)

[2] In Act III, sc. ii, Caliban says of Stephano and Trinculo:

> These be fine things an if they be not sprites.
> That's a brave god, and bears celestial liquor:
> I will kneel to him.

civilization must bring, of man's sense of his dependence on a transcendent world. What is primordial in man's nature is forced back by nature, culture, and authority; but the deep thing remains, however obscured. The brittle edifice of civilization, culture, and science cannot change it; and this we see if we look to the saints and the poets who break through the prison of sophistication in which many men find a delusory safety.

7

I fear that what I have said will appear extravagant. But if Shakespeare must make his Prospero something of a Virginia planter at bitter enmity with treacherous natives, and will not suffer him to speak of Caliban except in hatred and contempt, he was also aware that there was another side to the picture which he must not, however, allow Prospero to exhibit. Caliban himself must do that.

I quote now a few paragraphs from Hariot's *Briefe and True Report*:

Some religion they have alreadie, which although it be farre from the truth, yet beyng as it is, there is hope it may bee the easier and sooner reformed.

They beleeve that there are many Gods which they call *Montoac*, but of different sortes and degrees; one onely chiefe and great God, which hath bene from all eternitie. Who as they affirme when hee purposed to make the worlde, made first other goddes of a principall order to bee as meanes and instruments to be vsed in the creation and gouernment to follow; and after the Sunne, Moone, and Starres as pettie gods, and the instruments of the other order more principall. First they say were made waters, out of which by the gods was made all diuersitie of creatures that are visible or inuisible. . . .

They thinke that all the gods are of human shape, & therefore they represent them by images in the formes of men, which they call *Kewasowak* one alone is called *Kewas*; them they place in houses appropriate or temples, which they call Machicomuck; Where they worship, praie, sing, and make manie times offerings vnto them. In some Machicomuck; we have seene but on *Kewas*, in some two, and in other some three; The common sort thinke them also to be gods. . . .

They beleeve also the immortalitie of the soule, that after this life as soone as the soule is departed from the bodie, according to the workes it hath done, it is either carried to heauen the habitacle of gods, there to enioy perpetuall blisse and happinesse, or els to a greate pitte or hole, which they thinke to bee in the furthest partes of their part of the worlde toward the sunne set, there to burn continually. . . .

And this is the summe of their religion, which I learned by hauing special familiarity with some of their priestes. . . .[1]

I have said that it is difficult to believe that Shakespeare had not read Hariot's *Briefe and True Report*; and I call attention to Ariel's lines in Act III, scene iii:

> *You are three men of sin, whom Destiny*
> *That hath to instrument this lower world*
> *And what is in't,*

which recall Hariot's words, 'Who as they affirme when hee purposed to make the worlde, made first other goddes of a principall order to bee as meanes and instruments to be vsed in the creation and gouerment to follow; and

[1] D. B. Quinn, *Roanoke Voyages*, vol. i, pp. 372–5.

after the Sunne, Moone, and Starres as pettie gods, and
the instruments of the other order more principall.'
There is, then, 'one onely chiefe and great God, which
hath bene from all eternitie'; below this supreme Being
are the gods, his instruments; and these 'are of a human
shape'. Hariot's statement, coming from his visit to
Virginia as early as 1586, at the outset of the meeting of
Englishmen and Indians, has a classic importance; and it
was a statement of a witness of high and trained intelli-
gence.

But there is not only Hariot to bear this witness. There
is Strachey also. I said of Strachey's book, *The Historie of
Travell into Virginia*, that it provides in part his own
observation of the Indians; and in chapter 7 of the first
book, after speaking of the sacrificial practices of the
Indians, he goes on to say:

the great God (the priests tell them) who governes all the
world, and makes the Sun to shine, creating the Moone and
Starres his Companions, great powers, and which dwell with
him, and by whose vertues and Influences, the vnder earth is
tempered and brings forth her fruictes according to her sea-
sons, they calling Ahone, the good and peceable god, requires
no such dutyes, nor needes to be sacryficed vnto, for he entendeth all goode vnto them, and will doe no harme. . . .

This, again is a statement of the highest importance: it
was made by a man who was in Virginia from 1610 to
1611, still early days in the encounter of English and
Indian.

Strachey, indeed, failed to get his book published. He
began it in Virginia. He came home in 1611, and finished

it in 1612. According to Dr. Culliford, he probably returned in late October or early November. I have suggested that Strachey may have got back earlier, leaving Virginia on the *Elizabeth* in July. If so, he would have had time to talk with Shakespeare before *The Tempest* took final shape for its performance that autumn. However that may be, we need to remember that a number of distinguished Shakespearian scholars have believed that *The Tempest* was recast; and that it was recast for a performance at Court, in 1613, as part of the celebrations of the betrothal and wedding of the Princess Elizabeth and the Elector Palatine. If indeed Shakespeare recast the play for this occasion (and the play as we have it certainly suggests that it was written for a betrothal or a wedding), there would have been plenty of time for Shakespeare and Strachey to talk. In any case, there was enough in Hariot's *Report* for Shakespeare's purposes in rendering that other side of Caliban which Shakespeare must forbid Prospero to acknowledge; and for my part, I find it very hard to believe that Shakespeare and Hariot, who had in common so many friends and acquaintances on the Virginia Council, did not discuss, long and earnestly, what Hariot saw and learnt during his visit to Virginia, what, in particular, Hariot had learnt from the priests with some of whom he claimed a 'special familiarity'.

It is true that a sense of the 'one onely chiefe and great God which hath bene from all eternitie' was by no means the whole of Indian religion. There was another side of the religion of the Indians of which Hariot did not speak.

Increase Tarbox, in putting out in 1884 his *Sir Walter Raleigh and his Colony in America*,[1] reprinted Hariot's *Report*, and in a footnote (on p. 231) remarks on what Hariot said about the religion of the Indians:

Hariot with his kindly Christian nature and education has perhaps given a more elevated idea of the religion of the Indians than the case will bear. Doubtless, north and south, they did hold to the existence of the one Great Spirit and to a life beyond the grave, yet with these beliefs were joined such gross and cruel superstitions and revolting practices that one can find little pleasure in their religion.

Tarbox goes on to quote from John Smith's *Pathway to erect a Plantation*:[2] 'Some say, many of those nations are so brute that they have no Religion, wherein surely they may be deceived; for my part, I never saw nor heard of any Nation in the world which had not Religion, Deare, Bowes and Arrows. Those in *New-England*, I take it, beleeve much alike as those in *Virginia*, of many divine Powers, yet of one above all the rest. . . .' In this, Smith gives confirmation to what Hariot and Strachey said; but in his *Map of Virginia*, which was published in 1612,[3] Smith had written that 'the chiefe God they worship is the Diuell'; and Strachey confirms this (if, indeed, 'worship' is the right word) speaking as Smith did, of an evil God, Okeus, whom the Indians sought by sacrifice and other means to placate, and of whom they made

[1] Publications of the Prince Society, Boston.
[2] I give the quotation directly from Edward Arber's edition of the *Works* of John Smith, vol. 2, p. 939.
[3] *The Pathway* was published in 1631.

idols; Strachey then goes on to explain, as we have seen, that the Supreme Spirit, having the name of Ahone, 'who governes all the world' requires 'no such dutyes, nor needes to be sacryficed vnto, for he entendeth all goode vnto them'. It is not now to my purpose to speak of this other side of Indian religion which exhibits ritual directed to placating a 'god' of evil in the Universe and his subordinate evil spirits: but it seems clear that Setebos, the God of Caliban's dam, lived in a universe created and governed by a Spirit 'intending all good', and who had been 'from all eternitie'. Europeans through the centuries had feared evil spirits; so had the Indians. Setebos and Sycorax will serve to belong both to European daemonology and to the religion of the Indians; but for civilized Europe and primitive America alike, there was a great and good God who created and ruled the Universe.[1]

[1] For earlier accounts of Indian religion in Spanish America see Joseph Acosta's *Naturall and Morall Historie of the East, West Indies*, trans. E. G., London, 1604, Book V, esp. chapters 3 and 4; and Richard Eden's translation of the *Decades of Peter Martyr*, London, 1555, pp. 43–47 (Eden's translation of the *Decades* is included in Willes' *History of Travayle*). A later account of Indian religion in Virginia, of great value, is provided by Robert Beverley's *The History and Present State of Virginia* published in 1705. Beverley wrote from first-hand study of Indian religion, and confirms what Hariot and Strachey had said. See especially pp. 198–202, in Mr. Wright's edition of Beverley's book, Chapel Hill, 1947. For accounts of Indian religion by scholars of our own time, see J. R. Swanton's *The Indians of the South Eastern United States*, Washington, 1946, pp. 742–82; and Regina Flannery, *An Analysis of Coastal Algonquian Culture*, Washington, 1939, especially pp. 152–6. I add that Andrew Lang, who played so admirable a part in the development of the study of the history of religion, was well aware of the importance of Hariot and Strachey as students of Indian religion. See his *Myth, Ritual and Religion* (edition of 1899, with its preface).

8

I have been at some pains to say that, if we do not know and bear in mind, what Shakespeare learnt from Hariot, and very likely from Strachey also, about Indian religion, we can make little of Caliban's speech:

> *and sometimes voices,*
> *That, if I then had wak'd after long sleep,*
> *Will make me sleep again: and then, in dreaming,*
> *The clouds methought would open, and show riches*
> *Ready to drop upon me; that, when I wak'd,*
> *I cried to dream again.*

But there is, in all truth, another side to Caliban from what these lines show. There is Prospero's rendering of his nature; and in a marginal comment to some sentences of Strachey's recounting, in *A True Reportory*, the treachery and 'practices of villany' of the Indians we read: 'Can a leopard change his spots? Can a savage remayning a Savage be civill?'[1] Prospero's answer to the question is, No; Caliban will take no print of goodness, is capable of all ill. There came the moment in his cherishment of Caliban when Prospero said, *Thou shalt not*. Over against Caliban's dream of God and blessedness we must place his lust, his treachery, his resentment of authority and restraint, who was first his own king. Prospero was a king indeed. His authority in Milan had been usurped by evil; it may not be usurped in the island, as, in the end,

---

[1] *Purchas His Pilgrimes*, vol. xix, p. 62. I take the comment to be Purchas's. I do not forget that Purchas's *Pilgrimes* was not published until 1625.

it will not be usurped in Milan. Prospero's kingship must be sustained against evil here, as there; over primitive Caliban, as over civilized Antonio: always there is the concupiscence of lust, pride, and ambition of the world, warring against the vision of blessedness. This Prospero saw, as Caliban could not. The deep evil of our nature, resentful of continence and submission, goes along, in Caliban, with a sense of a transcendent glory; but the struggle between evil and blessedness is not joined in Caliban: how could it be? He is the natural man. In Antonio, evil has wholly triumphed, as it had in Goneril, Regan, Cornwall; he is less the natural man than Caliban. But Prospero sees what is at stake; it is only the spiritual man who sees clearly, and must suffer, the struggle; and in his jealousy for the spiritual, and in his sense of the fearful reality of evil, Prospero is harsh and intransigent to Caliban: Prospero is not only the Virginian planter; and the time will come when he will say: 'this thing of darkness I acknowledge mine'; as St. Augustine in his *Confessions* knew well the darkness that was in *him*, set over against the light before which he trembled in love and awe. Besides, Caliban sees Prospero differently in the end: 'How fine my Master is!' and says that he will seek for grace. But to this I shall return.

When therefore I said that we see in civilization a power which forces back man's natural sense of a transcendent reality, this is true only of the sophistication of the world; Prospero's sophistication is in the end the sophistication of the spiritual, whose nurture and authority are indeed necessary.

9

I began this chapter by referring to Sir Thomas More's *Utopia*. I conclude it by referring briefly to another Utopia: Bacon's *New Atlantis*, which was written in 1624. The ship which carried Bacon's travellers to New Atlantis was not shipwrecked. It had been driven up from Peru, and 'had rather met with calms and contrary winds than any tempests'. There were no storms off the coast of New Atlantis. The travellers had indeed been in great fear of their lives, having run out of supplies, 'in the midst of the greatest wilderness of waters in the world'; and 'were men cast on land, as Jonas was out of the whale's belly, when they were buried in the deep' (as, in *A True Declaration*, 'God that heard *Ionas* crying out of the belly of hell . . . pittied the distresses of his servants'). They were readily forgiven by the 'governor', on being shown so civilized, but so unknown, an island, for thinking 'this land a land of magicians, that sent forth spirits of the air into all parts'. But there were no magicians: only an ideal civilization, which had received the Christian revelation, with its Salomon's House, in which the study of the natural world was relentlessly and calmly pursued. There was no question of New Atlantis becoming a part of the Old World: its citizens saw to that. They only sent out every twelve years into the world three Fellows of Salomon's House, whose secret errand was to bring back 'knowledge of the affairs and state' of the old world, and 'especially of the sciences, arts, manufactures, and inventions of all the world; and withal to bring books, instruments, and patterns in every kind'. The rulers of New Atlantis were not to miss the advantages of scientific discoveries of the Old World; beyond that, there must be no contamination from 'civilization'. But in *The Tempest* there was never any question of not returning to Milan: the restoration of Prospero to power was the heart of the matter.

V

THE DREAM

I HAVE now spoken of Prospero, Ariel, and Caliban, and their histories. The play, so far as I have yet spoken of it, apart from the storm itself, is history only, or the telling of it. But the proper action of the play is now to begin; the long past is to be resolved: we are to move quickly to the play's ending—'the present business which is now upon us'. We shall see two conspiracies, the one, against Alonso, of Sebastian and Antonio, the other, against Prospero, of Caliban, Stephano, and Trinculo; and there will be the wooing of Miranda by Ferdinand and the masque which celebrates their betrothal. These three strands in the play's story, two of hate and murder, one of love and marriage, will come together in the last Act. There will be resolution then, and the return home.

But all that will happen will lead, we are aware that it must lead, to the restoration of Prospero to the throne of Milan. When he was Duke of Milan, Prospero cast the government of the State upon his brother Antonio; transported and rapt in secret studies and for the liberal Arts without a parallel, he grew a stranger to public affairs: he had been dedicated to seclusion and the bettering of his mind. We may be disposed to say that he could hardly be surprised if Antonio tried to seize for good the power that had thus been put into his hands: Prospero, after all, had neglected his plain duties. But it is also clear that Prospero will return to power. He cherishes indeed a deep sense of injury, of evil, and treachery carried out against him: but bountiful Fortune had now brought his enemies to the shore of the island; and his prescience and an auspicious star will return him to his throne. His return to the throne, as I have said, is the heart of the matter. His every third thought when Duke again may be of his grave; but we must assume that every first and second will be of Milan and its affairs: he will hardly neglect them again. His lines are:

> *and so to Naples,*
> *Where I have hope to see the nuptial*
> *Of these our dear-belov'd solemnized;*
> *And thence retire me to my Milan, where*
> *Every third thought shall be my grave.*

But we have no reason to take 'retire me to my Milan' as signifying a retirement from public duties. The word frequently signified in the sixteenth and seventeenth centuries, as the *Oxford English Dictionary* makes abundantly clear, the meaning of removing or betaking oneself merely: Prospero will leave Naples for Milan and his Dukedom. He will indeed meditate on death; he will not renounce his search for spiritual perfection and discipline. But it is not credible that he proposes to repeat his earlier mistake: of letting closeness and the bettering of his mind withdraw him from the duties which his station as Duke of Milan requires. Besides, we must be careful not to think of (or play) Prospero as an old man. He can hardly be that: when his brother dispatched him and Miranda twelve years earlier from Milan, Miranda was only three years old. The expectation of life in Shakespeare's time was indeed less than now, and Prospero can say, at one dramatic moment, 'my old brain is troubled'; but he is talking with Ferdinand and Miranda, who are little more than children, and he may well speak of himself to them in this way. But we must think of Prospero returning to Milan at the height of his powers, and addressing himself again, and with renewed energy, to the labours of government; and doing so not at all at the expense of the cultivation of his interior life. He returns as one to whom indeed great injustice had been done; but he returns also as one to whom great duties fall and of which he is not likely again to be forgetful. If we have become accustomed to think of Prospero as an elderly gentleman going into retirement, it is out of sentimentality only, because we are thinking vaguely of Shakespeare's last play and of his retirement to Stratford. But the truth is that the island has been a retreat for Prospero; and his return to Milan is a return to duty. The long holiday is over.

The return of Prospero to his dukedom provides, then, the end and purpose of all which is now to happen. Besides, Miranda, wronged with him, is to become the wife of Ferdinand, the heir to the throne of Naples; and Milan and Naples, united now through the collaboration of evil, will in future be united through the collaboration of love. It is no part of my purpose to review systematically all the sources, such as they are, of *The Tempest*. But one observation I must make. It has been observed that elements of fairy and folk tale run in *The Tempest*; the play draws on 'a vast reservoir of primitive fiction';[1] this is surely true. But I wish now to emphasize that it draws also on a vast reservoir of primitive history; I mean, on the traditional and mystical conception of kingship.

Everyone knows that royal authority and priestly function went along with each other in early days of human culture. It seems that the most simple and primitive types of society were democratic and gerontocratic; but the institution of divine kingship was to emerge with immense force in primitive thought and practice.

The divinity [said Sir James Frazer] that hedges a king was no empty form of speech, but the expression of a sober belief.[2] Kings were revered, in many cases not merely as priests, that is, as intercessors between man and God, but as themselves gods, able to bestow upon their subjects and worshippers those blessings which are commonly beyond the reach of mortals: Kings were therefore believed to possess magical powers, able to give rain or sunshine, make grow the crops, be bringers of life or death.

Prospero, the priestly king, will indeed abjure his magic, and bury his staff and book and not play the god; still,

[1] Mr. Kermode, in his Arden edition of *The Tempest* (Introduction, p. lxiii). Mr. Kermode is the most recent writer to call our attention to the 'presence of primitive elements in the deeply considered structure of *The Tempest*'; and he refers us to a valuable paper of W. W. Newell in the *Journal of American Folklore* (xvi), 1913, pp. 234–57, which studies these primitive elements and motifs as they have appeared in saga, fairy tale, and folk tale.

[2] It was so, for that matter, in England in the time of King James I.

he will return to Milan to resume his royal and priestly responsibilities.

Listen, now, to another passage from *The Golden Bough*:

The burdensome observances attached to the royal or priestly office produced their natural effect. Either men refused to accept the office, which hence tended to fall into abeyance; or, accepting it, they sank under its weight into spiritless creatures, cloistered recluses, from whose nerveless fingers the reins of government slipped into the firmer grasp of men who were often content to wield the reality of sovereignty without its name. In some countries this rift in the supreme power deepened into a total and permanent separation of the spiritual and temporal powers. . . .[1]

One might think that Frazer was writing a preface to *The Tempest*; and my purpose in quoting these words from his book is to illuminate further the end and object of the play, which is to return Prospero to his throne and, through Miranda, to enthrone his family in Naples also. As I have said, it is incredible that Shakespeare would have us believe that Prospero seeks to return to Milan to become again a cloistered recluse turning his back on government. On the contrary, we must believe, if the return to Milan is to make sense, that Prospero returns, chastened by his exile, which was also a punishment, to resume the full responsibility of government; he will reaffirm the dependence of the temporal on the spiritual and the deep identity of king and priest. I said at the end of the last

[1] *Taboo and the Perils of the Soul*, Sir James George Frazer, London, 1922, p. 17.

chapter that the 'sophistication' of Prospero is the sophistication of the spirit, and that without it the sophistication of culture and civilization is fragile and incapable of enduring. Prospero's return to Milan is his affirmation that this is so. The strain created between the discipline of the interior life and the desperate need of a culture (and, perhaps I may add, of that which we like to call 'Culture') for a spiritual basis for itself may be said to be a main theme of *The Tempest*.

2

It has been necessary to emphasize this conclusion to the play before beginning to speak of the action which follows upon the long story of things which happened long ago. The action begins, indeed, with the magic of Ariel and 'Come unto these yellow sands'; and with Ferdinand appearing, and speaking, as Miranda had spoken when she had first appeared, as in a trance. But of this and other features of this scene I shall speak later. I speak now of the threefold action: the two conspiracies, and then of Ferdinand and Miranda.

Of the two conspiracies, Antonio leads one: he will move Sebastian to kill his brother and assume the throne of Naples. He will have Sebastian do what he had done in Milan: the evil in Milan is to be repeated here on the island. Antonio and Sebastian believe Ferdinand to be dead, as they have long supposed Prospero to be. Sebastian will become absolute Naples, and Antonio absolute Milan: Antonio will render, with murder done, no tribute to Sebastian and Naples. Both would be kings. But also,

Antonio and Sebastian, empty of seriousness, take up
pages of the play with vapid, trivial, and cynical talk; the
goodness of Gonzalo is an occasion only of mockery to
them; they are incapable of reverence; and this is why
they are less *natural* than Caliban. Prospero will say that
Caliban is a born devil, or a demi-devil, at best; but the
noble conspirators are, Prospero says, worse than devils.

Caliban leads the other conspiracy. Not that he himself
would be king; he has indeed seen himself in the past as a dis-
placed monarch; but now he is willing enough for Stephano
to be the island's king; let him only murder Prospero. The
island is his, by Sycorax his mother, he had told Prospero;
but he will give it now to Stephano, as Antonio had in
effect given the kingship of Milan to Naples. In either
case, the end is kingship and power, whether, as we may
say, for the nobility or for the people: Antonio and
Sebastian would kill Prospero if they knew him for alive
in the island, as they plan to kill Alonso: Caliban and
Stephano will kill Prospero. But the kingship which will
in fact be affirmed and realized is not theirs, but Prospero's.

3

I turn now from the conspiracies to speak of the meeting of Miranda and Ferdinand and their wooing. I said
that, the long history of times past completed, Ferdinand
appears, following Ariel's music. He had appeared with
his father, Gonzalo, and Sebastian on the ship in the
storm; he had been, Ariel told Prospero, the first to leap
from the ship; and he did so shouting 'Hell is empty, and

all the devils are here'. But Ariel 'landed Ferdinand by himself'; and sitting on a bank, bitterly mourning his father's death, as his father was bitterly to mourn his, Ferdinand heard Ariel's music: if there were devils in the storm, there was music in the island which seemed to wait upon some god; these, like those Caliban heard, were not sounds which the earth owed.

I shall not now try to recount the meeting of Ferdinand and Miranda, guided and observed by Prospero, which then ensues. I remark only two things. First, when Prospero and Miranda watched the storm, Miranda had explained how she had suffered in seeing the brave ship, which had, no doubt, some noble creature in her, dashed all to pieces. Now the noble creature had appeared. Miranda did not know, she could not know, that Ferdinand was one of those who had been delivered from the storm and shipwreck: she could only think, as Caliban thought of Stephano, that he had dropped from heaven: he is not human and mortal, and she will not use the masculine pronoun:

> *What is't? a spirit?*
> *Lord, how it looks about! Believe me, sir,*
> *It carries a brave form. But 'tis a spirit.*

Then, when Prospero declares that Ferdinand is human, Miranda replies, with an exquisite collocation of genders:

> *I might call him*
> *A thing divine; for nothing natural*
> *I ever saw so noble,*

He is a god to her: she is a 'goddess' to him.

In the second place, it is to be noticed, I need hardly remark it, that from this point on, until the play's end and its final outbreak of wonder, Ferdinand and Miranda are kept away from the conspiracies. Prospero affects, in the discharge of his designs, a harshness to Ferdinand; he subjects him to Caliban's indignity of log-bearing; and he places his stern forbiddance of lust upon him, too. But of the evil that surrounds them and Prospero—Antonio's, Sebastian's, Caliban's, Stephano's—Ferdinand and Miranda remain ignorant, and in the end are told nothing or little of it.

4

We are therefore, from the moment Ferdinand and Miranda meet, divided between attention to the concupiscence and evil of the conspirators and attention to the innocence and love of Ferdinand and Miranda. This evil and this good appear scarcely to exist in the same world. So it may seem to us, the spectators. So it seemed, from time to time, we may say, to Prospero; and this we may illustrate from the most dramatic moment in a play which, for the most part, eludes the category of the strictly dramatic. Prospero is at last reconciled to Ferdinand, Ferdinand to Prospero; Stephano, Trinculo, and Caliban are moving with murderous intent towards the cell; the noblemen have been made desperate by the disclosure of their guilt. At this moment we turn, at the beginning of Act IV, to Prospero, Ferdinand, and Miranda. The marriage is to take place in Naples. But there is to be here now a masque of betrothal. First, there is Prospero's stern injunction of continence upon Ferdinand; then the incomparable beauty of the 'vanity' of Prospero's Art. As the majestic vision unfolds, Ferdinand says,

> Let me live here ever;
> So rare and wonder'd father and a wise
> Makes this place Paradise.

Then comes the speech of Iris,

> You nymphs, call'd Naiads, of the windring brooks,
> With your sedg'd crowns and ever-harmless looks,
> Leave your crisp channels, and on this green land
> Answer your summons: Juno does command:
> Come, temperate nymphs, and help to celebrate
> A contract of true love; be not too late.
> You sunburn'd sicklemen, of August weary,
> Come hither from the furrow, and be merry:
> Make holiday; your rye-straw hats put on,
> And these fresh nymphs encounter every one
> In country footing.

Then the dance. But towards its end, Prospero starts suddenly. Absorbed, like Ferdinand and Miranda in the masque's beauty, filled then, like them, with hope, love, joy, he had forgotten the beast Caliban, 'the minute of whose plot is almost come'. He breaks off the masque, is in a passion that 'works him strongly'; Miranda had never seen him so touched with anger, so troubled, so distempered. This is indeed the high dramatic moment of the play: in the face of the beauty of Ferdinand and

Miranda, their rescue from death and danger, their love and hope, their kingship and queenship to come, their innocence of the world's evil; and in face of the masque which celebrates and sets the seal upon their betrothal, there comes to Prospero the sudden thought of the wickedness of the world, the inexhaustible depths of human evil in places high and low. But the moment of drama is not over yet. What is dramatic in *The Tempest* is the drama of the interior life; as suddenly as before, Prospero's mind changes. He looks to Ferdinand and says,

> *You do look, my son, in a mov'd sort,*
> *As if you were dismay'd: be cheerful, sir.*

But it was Prospero himself who had been so moved, so dismayed; and now he is giving comfort to Ferdinand and Miranda who had been troubled only for his sake. These are the lines he then speaks:

> *Our revels now are ended. These our actors,*
> *As I foretold you, were all spirits, and*
> *Are melted into air, into thin air:*
> *And, like the baseless fabric of this vision,*
> *The cloud-capp'd towers, the gorgeous palaces,*
> *The solemn temples, the great globe itself,*
> *Yea, all which it inherit, shall dissolve,*
> *And like this insubstantial pageant faded,*
> *Leave not a rack behind. We are such stuff*
> *As dreams are made on; and our little life*
> *Is rounded with a sleep. Sir, I am vex'd;*
> *Bear with my weakness; my old brain is troubled:*

> *Be not disturb'd with my infirmity:*
> *If you be pleas'd, retire into my cell,*
> *And there repose: a turn or two I'll walk,*
> *To still my beating mind.*

The speech begins from the apparent serenity which suddenly succeeds his brief, fierce anger and dismay: 'be cheerful, sir'. He is anxious to allay the distress of Ferdinand and Miranda which he thinks must arise from the sudden apparent extinction of the beautiful beings who had been playing in the masque: but they were, he explains, as he had explained earlier, all spirits, returned now to their native element, the air, which they shared with Ariel, their master. Then he goes on to think of the masque's actors, and of the no doubt splendid 'spectacle' of the masque, in their transiency, as an image of human life and of the world, of the earth, and of all who inherit it. Then his thought moves forward to say,

> We *are such stuff*
> *As dreams are made on; and* our *little life*
> *Is rounded with a sleep.*

But it is clear that, in the utterance of these words, and no doubt in the utterance of the lines that precede and lead up to them, his earlier distress, which had caused him to dismiss the masquers, has returned; for he goes on at once to say:

> *Sir, I am vex'd;*
> *Bear with my weakness; my old brain is troubled:*
> *Be not disturb'd with my infirmity:*

If you be pleas'd, retire into my cell,
And there repose: a turn or two I'll walk,
To still my beating mind.

Vexations, trouble, weakness, occupy his beating mind. He had been anxious not to distress, but to comfort, the young, and did so—or sought to. But comfort for himself was harder to come by; and the words he began in order to comfort the young had served only to restore, or help to restore, his original distress.

What then shall we say? Prospero had played with the thought of human life as a masque, beautiful, majestic, transient: but it would not do. It is instead a bitter drama of good and evil: of Ferdinand and Miranda set over against Antonio and Sebastian; of Cordelia and Edgar set over against Regan, Edmund, Cornwall. The spirits who played the masque have, indeed, returned to their native air, as Ariel will shortly do. Prospero says,

We *are such stuff*
As dreams are made on, and our *little life*
Is rounded with a sleep.

He may keep up, so far as he may, the image of human life as a masque whose action must pass away, as no doubt the great world itself will pass away: but then, if what encompasses[1] our lives is the darkness of sleep, is this

---

[1] The traditional interpretation of these lines, illustrated for example, by the *O.E.D.* and Onions's *Lexicon* is that 'rounded' means 'finished off', 'rounded off' (with the suggestion, at least in the *O.E.D.*, of being thereby brought to completeness, to a certain perfection of form—as a sentence may be said to be 'rounded off'). I see that Mr. Kermode

'sleep' a name, a euphemism, for extinction; or is our life a 'dream' from which we shall awake to behold a world of reality incomparably more wonderful than it has entered the heart of man to imagine? This is the burden of the mystery which weighs upon Prospero's mind.

Hamlet, too, had meditated on life and death and dream:

> *To die, to sleep—*
> *No more. . . .*
> *'Tis a consummation*
> *Devoutly to be wished. To die, to sleep—*
> *To sleep—perchance to dream: ay, there's the rub,*
> *For in that sleep of death what dreams may come*
> *When we have shuffled off this mortal coil,*
> *Must give us pause. There's the respect*
> *That makes calamity of so long life. . . .*
> *. . . Who would fardels bear,*
> *To grunt and sweat under a weary life,*
> *But that the dread of something after death,*
> *The undiscover'd country, from whose bourn*
> *No traveller returns, puzzles the will,*
> *And makes us rather bear those ills we have*
> *Than fly to others that we know not of. . . .*

favours the interpretation of 'rounded' as 'crowned'; he derives this view from such lines as those in *A Midsummer Night's Dream*, where Puck says of Titania that 'she his hairy temples then had rounded with a coronet of fresh and fragrant flowers'; or again, from 'the hollow crown that rounds the mortal temples of a King'. But it seems better to take the word as meaning simply 'surround'. This fully meets the purposes of the quotations I have given; and *All's Well*, I. iii. 158; *Richard III*, IV. i. 60; and *Troilus*, I. iii. 196 bear out this view.

But now Prospero is saying that our life is such stuff as dreams are made of, ephemeral, unseeing, encompassed by sleep: the 'sleep' and the 'dream' are here and now, and our spirits and the 'masque' of life are to be dissolved into 'thin air'. Hamlet had thought he stood upon a firm ground of reality, and feared the dreams of a sleep to come; but now, true being is not here: we have only a dreaming life. 'The day it is that dreameth.'

But then it is not only Prospero who speaks of dream. Caliban does so, also. In his dreaming, the clouds he thought, would open and show riches ready to drop upon him; and when he waked, he cried to dream again. Here is his dream within his 'dream'; and we are here far from the dreams Hamlet had dreaded.

No doubt it is easy to take Prospero's lines at a certain face value, embodying a slight and trivial reflection suited to an Antonio or a Sebastian, for whom everything in the end is trivial; but it is right, within the full context and music of *The Tempest*, to take them for a reflection properly suited, not only to the author of *The Tempest*, but also to the author of *King Lear* who had cast Lear prostrate over the body of Cordelia:

> *Why should a dog, a horse, a rat, have life,*
> *And thou no breath at all? Thou'lt come no more . . .*

Prospero's words, and the vexation and distress, the weakness, and the beating mind which went with them are of the order of Keats's cry in his letter to his friend Charles Brown from the ship off Yarmouth, Isle of Wight, which was to take him to Italy and death: 'Is there another life?

Shall I awake and find all this a dream? There must be: we cannot be created for this sort of suffering'; and Prospero's every third thought will be of his grave.

5

I do not propose now to recount the scenes in the play which follow upon the masque: the discomfiture of Caliban, Stephano, and Trinculo in the filthy mantled pool, and the conclusion of 'the present business which is now upon us'. King, nobleman, the common man, primitive man, all are now to come before Prospero. The bitterness and anger he has felt against them all he will now put aside:

> *Though with their high wrongs I am struck to th' quick,*
> *Yet with my nobler reason 'gainst my fury*
> *Do I take part: the rarer action is*
> *In virtue than in vengeance: they being penitent,*
> *The sole drift of my purpose doth extend*
> *Not a frown further.*

Then with his resolve to forgive made and declared, come the lines abjuring his rough magic. I spoke earlier of Prospero's renunciation of magic. I need not now repeat what I said then. But I quote the great speech:

> *Ye elves of hills, brooks, standing lakes and groves;*
> *And ye that on the sands with printless foot*
> *Do chase the ebbing Neptune, and do fly him*
> *When he comes back: you demi-puppets that*
> *By moonshine do the green sour ringlets make,*

Whereof the ewe not bites: and you whose pastime
Is to make midnight mushrooms, that rejoice
To hear the solemn curfew: by whose aid,—
Weak masters though ye be—I have bedimm'd
The noontide sun, call'd forth the mutinous winds,
And 'twixt the green sea and the azur'd vault
Set roaring war: to the dread rattling thunder
Have I given fire, and rifted Jove's stout oak
With his own bolt; the strong-bas'd promontory
Have I made shake, and by the spurs pluck'd up
The pine and cedar: graves, at my command,
Have wak'd their sleepers, op'd, and let 'em forth
By my so potent Art. But this rough magic
I here abjure: and when I have requir'd
Some heavenly music,—which even now I do,—
To work mine end upon their senses, that
This airy charm is for, I'll break my staff,
Bury it certain fadoms in the earth,
And deeper than did ever plummet sound
I'll drown my book.

In place of magic, forgiveness comes now. Prospero's forgiveness does not come easily or readily. He needed to be instigated to it, we remark, by Ariel; and when he expresses it, he does so not without a touch of priggishness. Still, there is, we may think, more forgiveness than repentance. There is penitence enough in Alonso; and there is, perhaps, penitence in Caliban. There is little enough of it in Sebastian; there appears to be none in Antonio. Sebastian indeed exclaims, on seeing Ferdinand

and Miranda: 'A most high miracle'! But Antonio then and later shows signs neither of wonder nor regret. 'This thing of darkness I acknowledge mine', says Prospero of Caliban; but Antonio was a thing of far greater darkness, and was his own brother.

But by calling him his own, Prospero gives his pardon to Caliban, as he gives it to Antonio. Antonio exhibits a hard and hateful silence; Caliban says that he'll be wise hereafter and seek for grace: if he does so, what has been an elemental impulse to worship and a sense of dependency will become a 'wisdom', and an abjuration of right, and a supplication to Prospero for favour and all that that entails. Because this is so, on his nature Prospero's nurture will perhaps stick, after all. But Prospero speaks no soft or sentimental words to him, or about him: he is to clear up the cell and no doubt bring in more logs. 'Go to,' says Prospero, 'away!' Caliban may be wise hereafter and seek for grace; but certainly Prospero took little heed of Caliban's repentance; and only a minute earlier he had called him a demi-devil and a thing of darkness.

6

I said, at the outset of this lecture, that it is clear that all that will happen will lead to the restoration of Prospero to his throne. I wish now only to emphasize and illustrate further that this is so, and that all that happens falls within the contrivance of Prospero to the end of his return to power, however much he himself may be the instrument of Providence or Fortune, or of auspicious stars.

Prospero had come to the island, dispatched helpless with Miranda from Milan. Providence divine had guarded them; arrived there, Prospero finds Ariel and Caliban; and now, years later, bountiful Fortune has brought to the island Alonso, Sebastian, and Antonio, along with Gonzalo and Ferdinand. I recall the speeches, at the end of Prospero's long narrative to Miranda in the first Act:

Miranda: *And now, I pray you, sir,*
        For still 'tis beating in my mind, your reason
        For raising this sea-storm?

Prospero: *Know thus far forth,*
    By accident most strange, bountiful Fortune,
    (Now my dear lady) hath mine enemies
    Brought to this shore: and by my prescience
    I find my zenith doth depend upon
    A most auspicious star, whose influence
    If now I court not, but omit, my fortunes
    Will ever after droop: Here cease more questions.
    Thou art inclined to sleep; 'tis a good dulness,
    And give it way: I know thou canst not choose.

The course of Fate, or Destiny, is already plotted. 'I know thou canst not choose', says Prospero to Miranda as she falls into her sleep: but others cannot choose either, waking or sleeping: above all, Antonio must yield Prospero his dukedom. Besides, we are aware that the long past is to move quickly to its resolution, the nature of which, I have said, we know. Because this is so, *The Tempest* is hardly dramatic; or, as I have suggested earlier, it is chiefly dramatic in the incalculable twists and turns of

Prospero's mind as it staggers beneath the load of the destiny it carries and whose instrument he is.

I have previously spoken of the proper 'action' of the play as beginning with Ariel's *Come unto these yellow sands*, and leading in Ferdinand; and then I resisted speaking of this scene and its entrancement. But I must do so now. With the long preface, the preceding history over, at line 377 of Act I, scene ii, the play's action (for the storm and shipwreck belong less to the proper action than to the precedent events and circumstances) begins with Ariel, invisible (but visible, wearing a gown showing by convention that he is not so) playing and singing *Come unto these yellow sands*, invoking the kingdoms of the fairies, of the animals, and of the birds, and leading in Ferdinand. It was to the accompaniment of this music that the storm ceased: the tempest gives way to the music of Ariel, Prospero's servant-spirit; and this music Ferdinand follows and says,

> *Where should this music be? i' th' air or th' earth?*
> *It sounds no more: and sure, it waits upon*
> *Some god o' th' island. Sitting on a bank,*
> *Weeping again the King my father's wrack,*
> *This music crept by me upon the waters,*
> *Allaying both their fury and my passion*
> *With its sweet air: thence I have followed it,*
> *Or it hath drawn me rather. But 'tis gone.*
> *No, it begins again.*

I recall Miranda's lines,

> *If by your Art, my dearest father, you have*
> *Put the wild waters in this roar, allay them;*

and I put alongside them Ferdinand's

> *This music crept by me upon the waters,*
> *Allaying both their fury and my passion*
> *With its sweet air.*

But what 'action' is this, in any dramatic sense, whose beginning consists in the allaying of a storm by Ariel's music and which continues with Ferdinand (whose spirits as in a dream were all bound up, as he says later in the scene) using speech having these rhythms?

> *Sitting on a bank,*
> *Weeping again the King my father's wrack,*
> *This music crept by me upon the waters,*
> *Allaying both their fury and my passion*
> *With its sweet air: thence I have follow'd it,*
> *Or it hath drawn me rather. But 'tis gone.*

Or again,

> *The ditty does remember my drown'd father.*
> *This is no mortal business, nor no sound*
> *That the earth owes: I hear it now above me.*

Milton indeed was to listen carefully to these beautiful and most distinctive rhythms and use them in *Comus*: rhythms which are a form of movement arresting movement like Miranda's opening lines to her father, and constraining dramatic poetry, so far as is practicable, into the form of painting or sculpture: one is obscurely aware here of a meeting, a union, with other arts. (I do not doubt that we have to reckon with the masque as a form of art

which profoundly influenced Shakespeare's last creation.
But of this I shall speak later.)

My purpose now is to emphasize, if indeed it be necessary to do so, that all that happens is in Prospero's command:

> It goes on, I see
> As my soul prompts it,

Prospero says of the meeting of Ferdinand and Miranda;
and it will continue to go on so. 'Delicate Ariel, I'll set
thee free for this.' But it is not only Ferdinand's wooing
of Miranda which Prospero ordains and directs. Bountiful
Fortune has brought his enemies (along with Ferdinand
and Gonzalo, Stephano and Trinculo) to the island's
shores; and the two conspiracies he will also direct and
control. If we look to the conspiracy of Sebastian and
Antonio, it is Ariel who puts the rest to sleep—'they
dropped as by a thunderstroke'—to enable Antonio to ply
Sebastian's mind; and it is Ariel who then awakens the
others to prevent the murders of Alonso and Gonzalo,
the consequent kingship of Sebastian and the absolute
authority of Antonio over Milan. Later, Prospero will
bitterly upbraid them for a conspiracy he has carefully
aided. And if we look to the conspiracy of Caliban, we
recall the lines which Prospero speaks to call off the
masque:

> I had forgot that foul conspiracy
> Of the beast Caliban and his confederates
> Against my life: the minute of their plot
> Is almost come.

There was a time-table to his operations: all was laid
down. He had said to Ariel before the masque began:

> Go bring the rabble,
> O'er whom I give thee power, here to this place:
> Incite them to quick motion; for I must
> Bestow upon the eyes of this young couple
> Some vanity of mine Art: it is my promise. . . .

It does not matter whether the 'rabble' here means Caliban,
Stephano, and Trinculo, or Ariel's 'meaner fellows'.
Prospero was moving fast; his magic worked to the
accompaniment of fine time-tabling and delicate staff-
work; and if caught up in the masque of Ariel's making,
he forgot, or nearly forgot, the foul conspiracy of Caliban
and the minute of it, he thus only emphasizes to us the
extent and scope of his command. What alone are
intractable to him, or at best not readily manageable by
him, are interior and spiritual things: Ariel's longing to
be free, his own reluctance to forgive, Caliban's hatred of
him and his resolve, in which we may have doubtful
confidence, to seek his favour and be wise hereafter. For
the rest, the ordering of events and circumstances is at his
disposal.

Now because this is so, we may say that *The Tempest* is
less dramatic than theatrical; that it cannot properly be
said to have a dramatic action, for all is ordained and
presented; that, composed for the stage, it belongs essentially to what Wordsworth called the 'enthusiastic and
meditative imagination' rather than to what he called the
'human and dramatic imagination'. Wordsworth indeed

offers the works of Shakespeare as the most notable
illustration of the latter sort of imagination; and in
general this is indeed true in the highest degree. But of
The Tempest we may fairly say that it belongs to the
former, and is less dramatic than speculative and meditative.

7

I have been saying that we can speak of the action of
The Tempest only in an extenuated or rarefied sense. I
illustrate this further by returning briefly to what I said
in my second lecture about the storm which opens the
play. I said that there appeared to be two storms: one
which Miranda saw, or supposed she saw, which wrecked
and sank the ship and all its company. She had watched
helplessly. She had indeed been standing by her father
whose Art, she veritably believed, had raised the storm;
but she had been helpless to do more than utter her
distress when all was over and lost. When she spoke, she
spoke as one awakening from a dream, in which her
spirits (like Ferdinand's later) had been all bound up.

But there was, I said, another storm, the 'real' storm
which was Prospero's, not Miranda's. *This* storm was
raised, said Prospero,

> *in care of thee,*
> *Of thee, my dear one; thee, my daughter, who*
> *Art ignorant of what thou art, nought knowing*
> *Of whence I am.*

Miranda's storm, we may say, was seen out of ignorance,

or failure to understand, or confused vision; Prospero's
out of knowledge and power, and was by him

> *So safely ordered, that there is no soul—*
> *No, not so much perdition as an hair*
> *Betid to any creature in the vessel*
> *Which thou heard'st cry, which thou saw'st sink.*

The two storms, then, appear to belong to two different
orders of perception; and it is better, perhaps, to say that
in their differences they remind us of the incoherencies or
discords which we find in dreams; and what I said of the
physical circumstances of the viewing, by Miranda and
Prospero, of the storm may be judged also to illustrate
a certain pervasive, dreamlike quality of a play throughout which the words 'sleep,' 'waking', and 'dream' recur
again and again.

Besides, we reflect how differently the island itself
appears to its various beholders. To Prospero it is 'bare',
and to Ariel 'desolate': they both would be away from it.
To the child's eye of Caliban it is full of sights of tender
beauty as well as of terrible fear. To Gonzalo the grass is
lush and lusty and green, and the freshness of their clothes
a cause of astonishment; to Antonio the grass is tawny
and the freshness of their clothes either unnoticed or an
occasion for amused contempt. Alonso, in his grief for
Ferdinand, has eyes for nothing; and Ferdinand, in his
grief for his father, in his odd angle of the isle, also has
eyes for nothing, until his ears, led on by Ariel's music,
open his eyes to Miranda; and then he sees little else. To
each there is a private 'vision of the isle'. Of the island

itself we may say, with Gonzalo, 'Whether this be or not, I'll not swear'. There are too many 'subtleties' in it to 'let us believe things certain'.

I venture to suggest, in the light of all I have been saying about *The Tempest*, of the storm, of Prospero and his servants, of the island, of the play's action or lack of it, that we may best render the total impression it makes on us by saying that Prospero in truth never left Milan, and that the island and all that we see happen on it was a dream of Prospero's only. I must hasten to emphasize that in saying this I am proposing no doctrine or theory about the play in the sense that I think it was at all a part of Shakespeare's intention that we should think the action of the play a dream in Prospero's mind. This would clearly be false. I am doing no more than speaking in a way I think helpful to describe the reception of the play by our imaginations, and also, indeed, its fundamental character.

We may imagine Prospero, Duke of Milan, scholar and mystic, divided in his mind between the claims of government and affairs of state on the one side, and of study, contemplation, and divine pursuits on the other. Thus divided and distraught, he leaves many of the duties of state to his brother Antonio, whom he loves, but begins to fear and distrust. Then, in a dream, he sees the conspiracy of Antonio, and the fearful dispatch of himself and three-year-old Miranda (with Gonzalo incredibly suborned to aid the plot): the island; Ariel and Caliban; himself a magician commanding the elements; the ambiguous storm, the conspiracies, the betrothal of

Miranda and Ferdinand, and finally the return home. Then, when he awakes, there is still before him indeed the old, unceasing conflict between his responsibilities as head of the State and of his withdrawn, secret, divine life: from this conflict there will be no escape. Still, the dream had at last made clear the half-realized anxiety out of which it sprang. He has increasingly left affairs of state to Antonio; but he is aware in his deepest mind that the world's conflict is between, on one side, himself, the Priest-King, and on the other his brother who, he fears, knows no reverence in the face of the world, and acknowledges no 'deity in his bosom':

> *I feel not*
> *This deity in my bosom, twenty consciences,*
> *That stand 'twixt me and Milan, candied be they,*
> *And melt, ere they molest!*

In the end the choice is between himself affirming the spiritual sources of society, the dependence of the temporal and the secular upon the eternal and the sacred, and a society which rejects supernatural sanctions and in the event rejects morality itself. It is on this account that he must at all costs return to Milan; or, if we think of the play as dream only, he must give himself anew, now on his waking, to his duties, and resolve not to relax his grasp of the government of the State. Prospero calls Antonio and Sebastian worse than devils; they are corrupted into a positivism which removes morality from the world, erects power into a god, and calculation and self-seeking into a principle of action. As I have said earlier, in Caliban, primitive unsophisticated man, the lust of the world and the glorious sense of what lies beyond the world coexist; in the civilized mind of Antonio, there is only the lust of the world.

8

But if this be indeed the source of what I am calling Prospero's dream, we may also see the island as the sum of Shakespeare's dream of human life. Always there is the sea; it rounds our life, reverberates through it: sea-storm, sea-journey, sea-marge, sea-change; the sea mocking, requiting, never surfeited, threatening, merciful, tempestuous to begin with, calm in the end; and the island small and defenceless in the face of its illimitable and mysterious power. The symbolical value of the sea, we know, is inexhaustible. I do not myself find it possible to read *The Tempest* without recalling Keats's saying, in a letter written from the Isle of Wight in 1817, that Edgar's words in *King Lear* (a play also set upon an island) 'Hark! Do you not hear the sea?' had haunted him intensely;[1] and Keats was to write of the sea as priestlike and purifying round earth's human shores. Or we may think of Wordsworth's lines in the great O*de*:

> *Though inland far we be,*
> *Our Souls have sight of that immortal sea*
> *Which brought us hither.*

The sea indeed brings to Shakespeare's island all its characters, including Ariel and Caliban, the first the servant, the

---

[1] Keats misquoted. The line is 'Hark, do you hear the sea?'

second the child, of Sycorax; Prospero, in his affirmation of the dependence of the overt life of man and human society upon a rapt, secret, unworldly life; Antonio, aware only of worldly ends, without the innocence and poetry of primitive man, but having all his cunning and hatred; Ferdinand and Miranda, embodying the hope without which we could not live; and Ariel, not belonging to the earth, seeking release from the human, who yet touches Prospero's reluctant heart to forgive. There are others of whom I need not now speak. It is these who dominate Shakespeare's delineation, in the form of dream or summary symbol, of human life.

I have spoken of the role of the sea in the play: and the sea gives to the play a unity of place. It is always remarked that, in *The Tempest*, Shakespeare employs the unities of time and place. So far as he employs the unity of place (and if most of the action is before Prospero's cell, a lot of it is distributed over the island) he does so out of his desire to set a sea around the world. But it is certainly true that he employs the unity of time: and this is made clear to us. That he does so is not, I think we may be sure, to be explained either as a neo-classical gesture or as an accident; he does so out of a desire to provide, in his last play, by means of compression, greater definition; and precisely because, instead of wishing to satisfy any supposed conditions of drama, he wishes now to overcome, or put aside, the properly dramatic. Certainly, in *The Winter's Tale*, he had scattered the play's action extravagantly through space and time, but to an inevitable loss of its expressive power. He will now be classical and observe the unity of time in order to convey as conclusively as he can a sense of life not at all classical. This he is able to do by the long protasis; and by having at the play's centre a magician who ineluctably orders events (and events numerous and of great complexity) in time and thereby makes drama of little account. A dream having in it no contingency or uncertainty of issue, occupying a moment, or three hours, serves his turn now; and like a dream, the play has, along with a brittleness of surface and texture, a great depth and passion of meaning.

VI

THE MYSTERY

I

I SAID at an earlier stage that I would speak of *The Tempest* in relation to the masque-form; and it is convenient that I do so before I go further.

We know that *The Tempest* was acted on Hallowmas Night in 1611, in the Banqueting House in Whitehall, in the presence of the King. We cannot say for certain that this was its first performance; but it was probably a very early one. This is no place in which to resume the history of the masque. But it is appropriate to say that Twelfth Night 1605 saw the production of the first of the great masques in which Ben Jonson and Inigo Jones collaborated with scene-painters, composers, and choreographers to meet the insatiable demand at Court for display and pageant, accompanied by song and dance. This was the *Masque of Blackness*. In 1606 came *Hymenaei* celebrating the marriage of the Earl of Essex and Lady Frances Howard; in 1608 *The Masque of Beauty*; in 1608 also *The Haddington Masque* celebrating the marriage of Viscount Haddington to Lady Elizabeth Ratcliffe; in 1609 *The Masque of Queens*; in 1610 and 1611 there were masques for Prince Henry, *Prince Henry's Barriers* and *Oberon, the Faery Prince*; and in 1611 also a masque for the Queen, *Love Freed from Ignorance and Folly*. Therefore Shakespeare wrote *The Tempest*, late in 1610 or, more probably, in the course of 1611, with Ben Jonson at the height of his powers, bringing the masque-form to its brief apogee and writing some of his masques for the celebration of noble marriages. In 1608 the Quarto containing the masques of *Blackness* and of *Beauty*, both for the Queen, the one a sequel to the other, was published; in 1606 the Quarto of *Hymenaei*; in 1608 the Quarto of the *Haddington Masque*; in 1609 came the Quarto of *The Masque of Queens*. *The Tempest*, performed at Court on Hallowmas 1611, was repeated there in the winter of 1612–13—perhaps on 27 December 1612 to mark the betrothal of the Prince Palatine Elector to the Princess Elizabeth, to become known to history as Elizabeth of Bohemia. There are those who have believed that the betrothal masque of Ferdinand and Miranda was only now worked into *The Tempest* in honour of Princess Elizabeth's betrothal; others have thought that *The Tempest* was written for a betrothal in 1611 of which all record is lost. But in truth there appears to be no need for these speculations; we may fairly see *The Tempest* as the successor to *The Winter's Tale* (which was also revived at Court in the winter of 1612–13) in Shakespeare's new and last period of writing for the theatre: the two plays have enough in common; and *The Tempest* was probably played at the Blackfriars and at the Globe.

Still, it is true that the masque-form influenced the shaping of *The Tempest*. The masque was then so much required and so flourishing; if Shakespeare did not see Jonson's masques at Court, he can hardly have failed to read the Quartos; and these were years in which, according to lively tradition, Shakespeare and Jonson talked so much together at the Mermaid. Besides, in these years Shakespeare seemed to attach a quite special symbolical importance to the marriage of young royal personages. If only for these reasons we need not be surprised to see the influence of the masque at work in Shakespeare's shaping of *The Tempest*.

This is not to say that *The Tempest* is, in any sense, however recondite, a masque. Miss Welsford in her invaluable book, *The Court Masque*, speaks of *The Tempest* as illustrating a 'transmuted' form of the masque; but I venture to think that to speak in this way is perhaps misleading. It is enough to observe that certain features of the masque-form aided Shakespeare's purposes as he came to the creation of *The Tempest*.

In saying this, I do not have in mind chiefly Shakespeare's use of a betrothal masque in *The Tempest*, but certain more general considerations. The masque was not, we know, intended to be dramatic; it was, essentially, a dance of masqued dancers with courtly spectators: what came to precede the dance was, with varying degree of elaboration, monologue or dialogue or mythological or allegorical figures providing explanation of, or fanciful occasion for, the dance. In Ben Jonson's hands the preliminary dialogues were greatly developed, as we might imagine, and as we can see by a reading of those masques I have mentioned; but their dramatic content must remain slight enough: Milton's *Comus*, coming some twenty-five years later, is a more dramatic affair than any masque of Jonson's. Jonson might build up his dialogue as he would; but it must remain, no doubt to his annoyance, subsidiary to spectacle, music, and dance. Therefore, as I have said, little useful purpose is served by speaking of *The Tempest* as, in any sense, a masque: it is a far more elaborate and complex creation than any masque, and was indeed written in the first place for the popular theatre.

Still, I have been at pains to say that the dramatic quality of *The Tempest* is limited: all that happens in it is at Prospero's ordering; it is, in this sense, more something beheld than something suffered or worked through; it is something more presented than wrought by vicissitude and conflict. We may perhaps say that Prospero is here a presenter, as of a masque, that is, of a piece not embodying conflict and drama, but of something wholly prescribed and finished from its beginning. The long protasis leads on less to a dramatic action than to a spectacle unfolded, less to a development than to a symbol in which tense is overcome in order to exhibit the enduring features of the human condition.

Besides, there is the use of spectacle, and dance, and music. To speak of spectacle, there is the storm at the first: then later, for Caliban, Stephano, and Trinculo, the unleashing of the hounds; for Alonso, Sebastian, and the others, the astonishing show of the magic banquet, the monstrous shapes which accompany it and dance about it with gentle actions of salutation, and then Ariel as a harpy making it disappear; for Ferdinand and Miranda, the masque of betrothal. For dance, there is not only that of the spirits who accompany the banquet; there is the masque-dance of the nymphs and the sicklemen; besides, the long introduction over, Ariel leads in Ferdinand (and the play's action) with his invitation to the dance. Prospero is to break off the dance of the nymphs and the reapers in one of the dramatic moments of the play: drama here will arrest the masque. But Ariel's song, at the outset of the action, comes out of the spirit of dance transplanted from the court masque of the golden sands of Prospero's dream island.

Finally, there is more song and music in *The Tempest* than in any other of Shakespeare's plays: Ariel's music fills the air; but Caliban and Stephano have their songs, too, and Caliban his ethereal music. Music allays the waters and our passions, is the best comforter to an unsettled fancy. It is used to put to sleep and to awaken. Soft music accompanies the masque, and solemn and strange music the magic banquet. The winds sing to Alonso the name of Prospero; and the thunder, that deep and dreadful organ-pipe, pronounces it.

These then are some of the ways in which, we may believe, the masque lent itself to Shakespeare's purpose in his last play. At an earlier stage, I referred to the influence of *The Tempest* on *Comus*; we cannot doubt that it was profound. I have not time now to speak at length of it; I wished only to point to the undoubted influence of *The Tempest* on *Comus* as further evidence, if it were necessary, that something of the quality of a masque is indeed present in Shakespeare's play.

2

Before speaking of the masque and its influence on *The Tempest*, I had been speaking of Shakespeare's employment of the unities of space and time in his play; and I said, speaking of his employment of the unity of time, that a dream having in it no contingency or uncertainty of issue, occupying a moment, or three hours, served his turn now.

I wish, as I move towards the end of my discourse, to revert to this, to Shakespeare's compression into small compass of an elaborate work of art which, if it falls short of the dramatic in ways I have tried to show, was yet written to occupy three hours of time on a theatre's stage: a work of art of great complexity, fashioning much and greatly varied material, and having, in Mr. Kermode's phrase, 'a deeply considered structure'. We do not find, in Shakespeare's works, anything comparable, in form, to *The Tempest*.

Henry James wrote of *The Tempest*:

Such a masterpiece puts before me the very act of the momentous conjunction taking place for the poet, at a given hour, between his charged inspiration and his clarified experience; or, as I should perhaps better express it, between his human curiosity and his aesthetic passion. Then, if he happens to have been, all his career, more or less the slave of the former, he yields, by way of a change, to the impulse of allowing the latter, for a magnificent moment, the upper hand.

I quote James's words from Professor Kenneth Muir's *Last Periods*.[1] Like Professor Muir, I do not understand

[1] Liverpool University Press, 1961.

James's speaking of Shakespeare's slavery to human curiosity; but I understand, I think, his saying that *The Tempest* came out of, and matched, a fierce aesthetic passion.

Still, the phrase 'aesthetic passion' has an abstractness which invalidates it; or again, it will not do, I venture to think, to speak of Shakespeare's yielding momentarily to the 'impulse' of such a 'passion' after long 'slavery' to 'curiosity'. Indeed, I see the 'aesthetic passion', which James says gave birth to *The Tempest*, as being exerted now in exceptional degree as a sign of the consummation of the long journey of Shakespeare's imagination. I have, in these lectures, not spoken of the other plays of the last period: *Pericles* (so far as it was Shakespeare's), *Cymbeline*, and *The Winter's Tale*; I was anxious not to complicate a reading of *The Tempest* by using an elaborate framework of reference which might seem to reduce the play to the role of illustrating any inclusive doctrine or formula. But it is undoubtedly true that all four plays have certain features, which I do not now try to set out, in common; together they may truly be said to represent a last phase or period. But now, within this period, we see Shakespeare's imagination, in the last play of the group, making a final exertion to simplify and compress, and to establish in the play sharp limits, not in order to express a classical, but precisely in order to express a romantic, vision of life.

Shakespeare was not, then, as Henry James suggested, yielding to an impulse of aesthetic passion in reaction from 'curiosity'; he was exercising his creative powers in a way which matched the vision to which in these plays, but

above all in *The Tempest*, he had come. The long period
of exploration (what Henry James calls 'curiosity') was
now over; and we may indeed follow Henry James in
saying that the masterpiece of *The Tempest* puts before us
'the very act of conjunction taking place for the poet, at
a given hour, between his charged inspiration and his
clarified experience': Henry James's first description of
what we see in *The Tempest* is better, we may believe,
than his second, with its talk of curiosity and impulse
yielding to passion.

The severity and economy of the form which Shakespeare gave to *The Tempest* comes, then, from a certain
finality and confidence succeeding the labours of his
imagination in the tragedies which I have illustrated in
speaking of *Hamlet* and *King Lear*; from the light and
peace of the 'clarified experience' which followed, and
could only have followed, the darkness and tumult of
the tragedies. Where earlier he was seeking, he is now
showing; and in the intensity of his vision, his experience
thus 'clarified', his sense of life clear after long uncertainty,
he experiences also the greatest intensity of what Henry
James calls the 'aesthetic passion:' the 'aesthetic passion'
was strongest and purest at his moment of farewell to the
theatre and when, like Ariel, he was anxious to be off.
It is true enough, as I have said, that he could come by the
great technical triumph we find in *The Tempest* only
through the creation of a Prospero for his central character; but then, this was the point at which he required,
to convey his final vision, the action of an irresistible
magician.

3

At the outset of these lectures, I said that I would be on
my guard against a temptation to allegorize *The Tempest*.
I said, too, that we are conscious in reading *The Tempest*
that (like indeed the other 'Romances') it seems heavy
with what, for want of a better word, I called 'doctrine';
but I also said that Shakespeare observes and sustains a
certain reticence which it is essential to respect. I wish to
speak briefly again now of allegory and doctrine in *The
Tempest*.

I do not think we can deny the presence of allegory in
The Tempest. I have in mind the figure of Prospero in the
second scene of the play in his conversation with Miranda:
he appears there to represent, in his relation to Miranda,
a benign, even a Christian, Providence; and this I sought to
convey in speaking of this scene. Still, when this has been
said, it is also certainly true that this is not the whole of the
story about Prospero. Once the action of the play has
begun, and Prospero is seen in active relationship with
Caliban, Ariel, and the others, he is certainly no longer
chiefly apprehended as a divine Providence, but as very
human: continuing indeed to order all things, still, within
the action of his own contriving, irascible, anxious, loving,
hating, intolerant, reluctant to forgive.

Now this representation of a very human Prospero
throughout the action of the play was inevitable; to have
represented him as a divine figure, or as a saint, in his
dealings with the other characters of the play, would have
been (apart from any question of censorship) both im-

practicable and in bad taste. Even Shakespeare could no more have managed it than the rest of us; he was a working dramatist and was writing for a Jacobean theatre, which was not only secular but viewed by most Christian people with detestation. Shakespeare then renders to us a Prospero whom we cannot fail to see both signifying a divine Providence and possessing certain clear human infirmities. We marvel at the skill with which Shakespeare effects this union: even in the scene (the second of the play) where the sense of Prospero as a superhuman Providence comes most strongly to us, we are already made aware of him, in the peremptoriness he shows to Miranda, as the figure of mortal weakness he is to be throughout the play's action.

But I remark another feature of Shakespeare's presentation, later in the play, of Prospero. I have been saying that, in the second scene of the first Act, the sense of Prospero as signifying a superhuman Providence is very strong in our minds, but that later in the play our sense of him as merely human, in spite of all his magical powers, grows steadily stronger. Now it is to be observed that in Act III, Scene iii a doom is pronounced upon the evildoers. They have been rounded up. There is then solemn and strange music; and there is Prospero 'on the top, invisible'. There enter several strange shapes, who bring in a banquet, and dance about it with gentle actions of salutation, and invite the King and the rest to eat. Then, when, after their astonishment and hesitation, they are about to do so, the banquet vanishes through the action of Ariel, in the guise of a harpy; and now Ariel—not

Prospero—pronounces judgement upon the wrongdoers.
Here is his speech, made with Prospero 'on the top,
invisible':[1]

> *You are three men of sin, whom Destiny,—*
> *That hath to instrument this lower world*
> *And what is in't,—the never-surfeited sea*
> *Has caus'd to belch up you; and on this island,*
> *Where man doth not inhabit,—you 'mongst men*
> *Being most unfit to live. I have made you mad;*
> *And even with such-like valour men hang and drown*
> *Their proper selves.*

Alonso, Sebastian, etc., here draw their swords

> *You fools! I and my fellows*
> *Are ministers of Fate: the elements,*
> *Of whom your swords are temper'd, may as well*
> *Wound the loud winds, or with bemock'd-at stabs*
> *Kill the still-closing waters, as diminish*
> *One dowle that's in my plume: my fellow-ministers*
> *Are like invulnerable. If you could hurt,*
> *Your swords are now too massy for your strengths,*
> *And will not be uplifted. But remember,—*
> *For that's my business to you,—that you three*
> *From Milan did supplant good Prospero:*
> *Expos'd unto the sea, which hath requit it,*
> *Him and his innocent child: for which foul deed*
> *The powers, delaying, not forgetting, have*
> *Incens'd the seas and shores, yea, all the creatures,*

[1] See Professor Kermode's Arden Edition, p. 155, for a discussion
of the production of this scene and the location of Prospero in it.

Against your peace. Thee of thy son, Alonso,
They have bereft; and do pronounce by me
Ling'ring perdition—worse than any death
Can be at once—shall step by step attend
You and your ways; whose wraths to guard you from,—
Which here, in this most desolate isle, else falls
Upon your heads,—is nothing but heart-sorrow
And a clear life ensuing.

Here is Ariel, pronouncing divine judgement and em-
ploying, in doing so, the Christian categories of sin,
perdition, and repentance (which Ariel calls 'heart-
sorrow'). But he also speaks of Destiny—a Destiny
which 'instruments this lower world'—of Fate, and of
'the powers', and clearly avoids any explicit statement of
a Christian Providence or Judge. There is here a careful
ambiguity. Besides, we may feel a certain discomfort at
Shakespeare's making Ariel, a daemon of the air and an
unhuman creature not belonging to any Christian
hierarchy, the mouthpiece (however carefully briefed by
Prospero)[1] of this doctrine; as we may feel a certain discomfort at the thought of Prospero, sitting on the top, invisible (no doubt on an upper stage), and referred to by
Ariel when he says

> *The powers, delaying, nor forgetting, have*
> *Incens'd the seas and shores . . .*

Further, Ariel speaks his judgement in the shape of a

---

[1] See III. iii. 85:

> *Of my instruction hast thou nothing bated*
> *In what thou hadst to say.*

harpy, and thereby recalls Celaeno polluting the banquet
of the Trojans on the Strophades. No doubt Shakespeare
felt some hesitancy in giving the speech to Ariel un-
disguised: Ariel does not lend himself readily to a moral-
izing or religious role; and the disguise Shakespeare and
Ariel resorted to was a classical one, that of a Harpy
envisaged as a minister of divine vengeance. Here then
a tetrarch of the air, however transformed by Shakespeare's imagination, speaks words of Christian meaning
in the guise of a classical figure. Mr. Seznec speaks[1] of the
'fragile harmony' which, at its apogee, the Renaissance
effected between the spiritual values of Christianity and
a pagan cult of life. We see here, in this scene of which
I speak, early in the seventeenth century in England,
what we can only call a brittle conjunction—I do not say
harmony—of the modern, the medieval, and the classical.
It leaves us somewhat uneasy; no doubt it left Shakespeare
uneasy too.

Prospero here again then appears (in his invisibility) as
a Providence ordering all things. But it needs to be
remembered that this scene is not necessary for what is
properly the play's action; it is not of the same order, in
any point of view, as the scene at the beginning of Act V,
where Prospero, as Duke of Milan, confronts those who
had offended against him; here Prospero, upbraiding and
forgiving those who have wronged him, renders the past
not at all in religious terms, as Ariel's harpy had, but in
wholly human ones: he is the Duke of Milan merely,
reclaiming his own. He declines to give the whole story:

[1] In *The Survival of the Pagan Gods*, Harper, New York, 1961.

For 'tis a chronicle of day by day
Not a relation for a breakfast, nor
Befitting this first meeting;

and he leaves them wondering.

Now earlier, in the great second scene of the first Act, in which Prospero makes his narration to Miranda, Prospero appears wonderfully to unite in himself a divine and a human role. Later in the play the two roles appear to exist in clear separation from each other.

But having thus far allegorized Prospero, and allowed that he seems, with one part of him, to signify a providential and supernatural power; and allowing that Shakespeare slyly saw himself in Prospero: the god, the poet, and the man obscurely joined in one; having allowed this we cannot say that there is further allegory to be detected in the play. We may indeed see in the creation of Caliban a certain generalizing intention: Caliban as primitive man and then the impact of civilization upon him, his mingled innocence and sophistication. But to say of Caliban that he is an allegorical figure is to stretch the word beyond its proper use; and it is not possible to allegorize Ariel into anything: into what? Shakespeare would have laughed at our question: there is no answer to it. We may speak of allegory in the play only in regard to Prospero so far as he stands, as he certainly appears at time to do, for supernatural power: but the dichotomy which allegory requires between signified and signifying Shakespeare plays down in his creation of Prospero, so far as he can: he seeks, even there, and achieves, a proper obscuration of his purpose.

He was, as I have said, writing for the theatre, not composing an allegorical preface to a dance.

Still, it is also true that we are aware that Shakespeare in *The Tempest* has come to the very limits of theatrical secular art, and of his pressing hard against them. I have spoken of the island and the sea as symbols of great power and significance in the play and as parts of Shakespeare's deepest intention here. I have also, at certain places in what has gone before, explicated the 'doctrine' which seems to me certainly contained within the seamless, if strained, texture of the play; or again, as in speaking of Prospero's great speech at his breaking-off of the masque, I have provided interpretation, according best with the rest of the play, where Shakespeare, as I believe, was deliberately ambiguous or unexplicit. To do this requires a certain disloyalty to what I have called Shakespeare's reticence in his last plays and certainly not least in his last play. But this reticence was perhaps as constrained as it was chosen. The expression of the sense of life to which he has now come must be contained within the theatre; it must hold a stage. If only for this reason, what now Shakespeare saw must remain at best half-disclosed, an arcanum as much obscured as revealed, a mystery. He was aware that what now possessed his mind was beyond the power of his art to convey, or of any audience in the world to receive. He knew now, in a new and special sense, that the best in this kind are but shadows. He had his mystery, his closeness, too; and his art must partake of a certain 'secrecy' and concealment.

4

I spoke in my first chapter of *Hamlet* and *King Lear*; and
to them I must return briefly and relate them to what I
have been saying about *The Tempest*. I said that in *Hamlet*
Shakespeare compassionately observed the deep perplexity
of the modern mind: he was indeed prophetic and rendered
the agony to come. But he comes, within the compass of
some five years, to the composition of *King Lear*. In *King
Lear* we see him contemplating the extremity of evil in
Goneril, Regan, Cornwall, and also the suffering and
deaths of Cordelia in her transcendent goodness and of
Lear in his commonplace and then redeemed humanity.
I said that Shakespeare was resolved to give the goodness
of Cordelia and of Edgar, and of Lear at the end, no
mitigation of its suffering; and in the face of the terrible
deaths of Cordelia and Lear we are brought to say in truth
with Kent that all here is 'cheerless, dark, and deadly'. There
is no comfort here. But I also said there is no demonstrable
reading of the play any more than there is of life itself;
and there are three things in it: the extreme suffering,
helplessness, and then apparently hopeless defeat of love;
the figure of Cordelia, as almost one of heavenly grace;
the innocence to which Lear came when he found
Cordelia again; these are things which may cause us to
think that Shakespeare was perhaps looking beyond the
world a tragic dramatist—at least under the conditions in
which Shakespeare was working—can attempt to render.
We may hold that here Shakespeare was determined to
confront himself and us—in the extreme—with the silence

and darkness to which the world must bring us; that therefore the play itself brings us to a waiting and a hope for what lies beyond the world. But this hope cannot live within the play itself; within the play all is indeed cheerless, dark, and deadly. In *King Lear* we may say that we are at the world's end. 'Is this the promis'd end?' says Kent, seeing Lear carry in the dead Cordelia; and Edgar replies, 'Or image of that horror?'

It is from this point that we move on to *The Tempest* as I have shown it. Shakespeare wrote much between *King Lear* and *The Tempest*. About the time of *King Lear*, Shakespeare wrote (at least, parts of) *Timon of Athens*. The dating of the tragedies, everybody knows, presents difficulties; but there is a substantial amount of evidence that *Macbeth* succeeded *King Lear*; and that *Antony* and *Coriolanus* probably preceded the 'Romance' group. I do not here attempt to describe the passage of Shakespeare's mind from *King Lear* to *The Tempest*: I only take *King Lear* as the darkest and most terrible of the tragedies in which, in Keats's phrase about Milton, Shakespeare 'committed himself to the Extreme': and I have tried to show to what, in *The Tempest*, he came.

It will be clear from what I have said that Shakespeare, in *The Tempest*, does not at all exhibit human life as no longer tragic. The tragic sense of life is not something which can be put away, or an illness of which one may be cured; and the 'promised end' is not to be put off. It is true to say of *The Tempest* that all ends happily. Antonio and Sebastian will not reign in Milan and Naples: Ferdinand and Miranda will do that. But we shall not, if we are wise, or better, if we attend to the music of *The Tempest*, take this to signify mankind's release from days few and evil. Bacon had certainly thought that there lay to our hands the means whereby we might deliver mankind from its wretchedness; we might soon usher in the Kingdom of Man. We now, three hundred and fifty years later, see the Kingdom of Man for the artificially lit, brittle, nightmarish, self-destroying thing it is, a scientific 'culture' divorced from the spirit of man. This is how Bacon's dream has turned out. It has no part in Prospero's dream of the future, and no part in Shakespeare's. We may not take Ferdinand and Miranda and their future reigns to signify the coming of a brave new world and a happy Kingdom of Man. Disillusion will come to them too. There are, and always will be, the Antonios and Sebastians, frivolous, without reverence, treating the prompting of their moral natures as irrational, delusory, or meaningless; Caliban's words: 'I'll be wise hereafter and seek for grace' have no great ring of truthful prophecy about them; and Prospero himself is oppressed, and his mind made to beat, with the thought of the human evil and misery which he did not imagine, with all his magic, he might erase. There will always be Gonzalo too, and a great store of human kindness. But of Ferdinand and Miranda we shall say, if I may risk allegorizing them, that they represent the hope by which we live and without which we could not bear the burden of our lives.

But we cannot say that Shakespeare's last play comes to us in any rosy glow of cheerfulness, or of confidence in the future of mankind. *The Tempest* does not blot out the deaths of Gloucester and Cordelia, or the unspeakable evil of Edmund, Cornwall, Goneril, and Regan: there is Antonio, who knows no deity in his breast, and Caliban, who has learnt language from Prospero only to curse him. It is natural to feel a great deal more sympathy with Lytton Strachey in his essay on Shakespeare's final period than with those who see *The Tempest* as a comfortably and happy conclusion to the drama of Shakespeare's life. But also, if what I have been saying has any truth, we find in *The Tempest* sources and modes of feelings far profounder than can be contained within the compass of humanitarian optimism or of Lytton Strachey's anxious bitterness. I do not now propose to summarize what I have said earlier: about Prospero as Providence, as a scholar and magus dedicated to closeness and the bettering of his mind, whose every third thought will be his grave; his return to the throne and his overthrow of merely secular power; then of his sense of life as a dream surrounded by a spiritual order of which Caliban too has his vision; of the island and the sea; of Shakespeare's creation here, though composed for the theatre, transcending the dramatic: of all this I say no more now and come to Prospero's epilogue.

5

Here they are, Shakespeare's last words to an audience which was to be of a magnitude of which he could have entertained no conception.

> *Now my charms are all o'erthrown,*
> *And what strength I have's mine own,*

Which is most faint: now, 'tis true,
I must be here confin'd by you,
Or sent to Naples. Let me not,
Since I have my dukedom got,
And pardon'd the deceiver, dwell
In this bare island by your spell;
But release me from my bands,
With the help of your good hands:
Gentle breath of yours my sails
Must fill, or else my project fails,
Which was to please. Now I want
Spirits to enforce, Art to enchant;
And my ending is despair,
Unless I be reliev'd by prayer,
Which pierces so, that it assaults
Mercy itself, and frees all faults.
As you from crimes would pardon'd be,
Let your indulgence set me free.

These beautiful lines are pervaded by so exquisite an ambiguity that I must, for my conclusion, speak briefly of them. Prospero steps out from the play in which he has been the central character. He speaks now as the actor still in the garb of Prospero; at the same time he is no doubt the voice of the author. As actor and author in one, he declares himself no Prospero having power to enchant his audience and compel their plaudits. Instead, he is in *their* power, and he beseeches their favour: it is now they who hold and cast the spells, not he. Let them dispatch him home by the magical powers of their applauding hands: their favourable breath must waft him there. Compulsion he no longer owns; he can only pray his audience's mercy, and ask its forgiveness for his faults, whether as actor or dramatist, or both. As they would be forgiven for their faults, let them forgive his imperfections, and set him free.

But in and through all this, which belongs perfectly to the setting of the stage of the Blackfriars or the Globe, there is woven that which belongs to no theatre and to no play. He has rejected his magic, broken his staff, drowned his book. Power over the spirits, the enchantment of his art, he has abandoned; formerly a god, setting roaring war betwixt the green sea and the azure vault, or plucking up pine and cedar, he is now human only, and weak, as he always was. The magic was only play-acting. But Prospero is also the mind of European civilization casting off the shackles, and the false hopes, and the terrors of magical daemonology. Only prayer supplicating Divine Mercy can provide absolution and strength. The choice is between despair and prayer. What could not be said in the play may be said in the Epilogue. But even here, because of the teasing ambiguity in which the Epilogue is conceived and uttered, we are not far away from elusiveness, and a certain shadowing of a secret, and of a mystery.

PRINTED IN GREAT BRITAIN
AT THE UNIVERSITY PRESS, OXFORD
BY VIVIAN RIDLER
PRINTER TO THE UNIVERSITY